The 2003 OCLC Environmental Scan:
Pattern Recognition

A report to the OCLC Membership

The 2003 OCLC Environmental Scan:
Pattern Recognition

A report to the OCLC Membership

Principal contributors:
Cathy De Rosa
Lorcan Dempsey
Alane Wilson

Editor:
Alane Wilson

Graphics and layout:
Rick Limes
Linda Shepard

OCLC Online Computer Library Center, Inc.
Dublin, Ohio USA

Further details may be obtained from the OCLC Library &
Information Center at: information_center@oclc.org

Printed in the United States of America

Cataloged in WorldCat® on December 19, 2003
OCLC Control Number 53934212

ISBN: 1-55653-351-9

09 08 07 06 05 04 | 1 2 3 4 5 6

Thanks to the many OCLC staff
who contributed in a wide variety of capacities,
from research to editing to interviewing
for this report.

Contents

vii   The Landscape: Overview

1   Purpose, Scope & Notes on Methodology

3   The Social Landscape

15   The Economic Landscape

33   The Technology Landscape

53   The Research & Learning Landscape

69   The Library Landscape

97   Future Frameworks

107 Appendices

    109   OCLC

    113   Glossary

    125   Collections Grid

    127   People Consulted

    133   Readings & Sources

    149   Notes & Ideas

The Landscape: Overview

"...[W]hat we conceive about our business is not sufficient to fully understand all the effects that are actually happening in and around our business....[W]e are completely unable to perceive of all the dynamics of our business environment because our conception limits our perception. Our accumulation of, and intense focus on, our knowledge controls what we believe. And, what we believe controls what we are able to see. What haven't you noticed lately?"[1]

Change has become a cliché, a worn-out concept that has lost its power to inform. At the same time change continues to be a constant—and, indeed, what would be the alternative?

Nevertheless, we are sure that rapid transformations, particularly in the technological sphere of the public world, are more profound and more frequent than at any other time in humanity's history. Whatever occupation we hold, the day-to-day reality of our workplaces is change. But "change" is made up of so many events, inventions, ideas, replacements, introductions, alterations and modifications that the complexity of the environment overwhelms vocabulary. We are reduced to clichés and, in attempting to identify and understand all changes as they affect our environment, become less able to notice what we haven't noticed.

Google is disintermediating the library.

Content Vendor

Let us accept, then, that change is profound, accelerating, transforming and unpredictable. And let us also accept that, absent the talents of the Oracle of Delphi, any person or organization is unlikely to be able to make meaningful predictions that are helpful for charting directions for an indefinable future.

An example close to home will suffice: Arthur D. Little wrote a 90-page environmental scan for OCLC and the OCLC Board of Trustees in 2000. There is not one mention of the phenomenon that profoundly changed the "infosphere" because this phenomenon had just entered that space. In the subsequent three years, Google has become ubiquitous, the major player in search technologies, and often a substitute for a visit to the local library's reference desk.

1. Mark Federman, Chief Strategist, McLuhan Program in Culture and Technology, University of Toronto, *Information Highways Conference 2003*, Keynote Speech delivered March 25, 2003, www.mcluhan.utoronto.ca/EnterpriseAwarenessMcLuhanThinking.pdf.

Trying, then, to grasp the essence of the changes that impact the complex, interrelated set of organizations that make up OCLC's world is like fractal geometry. The closer the analysis, the greater the complexity of the overall picture. In other words, it is easy to become bogged down in analyses of what libraries, archives, museums and allied organizations might need to do and become and so, then extrapolate what OCLC needs to do and become. The sheer volume of large, significant changes to the environment overwhelms, and inertia or endless discussion can be the result. However, the appearance of the next "Google" in a month will twist the lens of the kaleidoscope and the image under examination will change completely.

OCLC's beginnings and subsequent successes were predicated on an understanding of the environment of the time, and on the bold, not minor or incremental, introduction of a service that many librarians did not even see a need for. OCLC created and led a revolution based on the inspired linking of technology with collaboration in the early 1970s.

Profound as this was, the introduction of shared cataloging was a revolution inside the walls of the library. The immediate effect on the users of libraries was not large, especially before the introduction of automated interlibrary loan (another inspired linking of technology with collaboration). The use of highly structured, standardized metadata to organize content and inventory organizational assets did not migrate much beyond the library. Indeed, it did not migrate in any significant way into the sister organizations of archives and museums.

At the same time that Fred Kilgour was developing his idea for a shared, computerized catalog, "Lick" Licklider, at the U.S. Department of Defense's Advanced Research Projects Agency, demonstrated 40 computers connected together in a network called ARPANET. He predicted that by the year 2000 millions of people would be online connected to one another and to information by a global network. He called it the Galactic Network.

In 1984, William Gibson's novel *Neuromancer* was published and introduced the terms "cyberspace" and "matrix" to refer to "a consensual hallucination experienced daily by billions [...] A graphical representation of data abstracted from the banks of every computer in the human system. Unthinkable complexity. Lines of light ranged in the nonspace of the mind, clusters and constellations of data. Like city lights, receding..."[2] In 1990 Tim Berners-Lee developed a program that allowed a real world matrix to develop. He called it the WorldWideWeb.[3]

It might not be overstating the case to say, only 13 years later, that the Web has became the most significant engine driving changes that impact OCLC and its member and participant institutions. It would be hard to find a person working at OCLC or in a member organization whose professional and personal life had not been affected by the Web.

Whatever the benefits to personal lives, the ubiquity and ever-present nature of the Web and the billions of pages of content accessible in this matrix of information are both boon and bane. There is a subdued sense of having lost control of what used to be a tidy, well-defined universe evident among those

> *"Are we automating nineteenth-century librarianship?"*
>
> **Fred Kilgour, 1977**

---

2. William Gibson *Neuromancer* (New York: Ace Books, 1984): 51.
3. Tim Berners-Lee, *WorldWideWeb: proposal for a hypertext project*, November 12, 1990, www.w3.org/Proposal.html.

who work in this information environment. Many are pessimistic, some are optimistic, but one theme persists: The landscape has changed and the maps have not been published yet.

It has become increasingly difficult to characterize and describe the purpose of and the experience of using libraries and other allied organizations. The traditional notions of "library," "collection," "patron" and "archive" have changed and continue to change. The relationships among the information professional, the user and the content have changed and continue to change.

What has not changed is the implicit assumption among most librarians that the order and rationality that libraries represent is necessary and a public good. So there is a persistent and somewhat testy tone to much that is written about the changed information landscape by those in the information community: Why don't "they" get it that libraries and librarians are useful, relevant and important in the age of Google?

This too shall pass. The constant questioning of a library's reason for existing is a very good thing. Libraries have continued to evolve to find their appropriate function—their core service. They will continue to get funded and continue to exist.

Director, OCLC Network

Simplistically, libraries and archives came into being to provide a central location for hard-to-find, scarce, expensive or unique material. Scarcity of information is the basis for the modern library. In countries where information continues to be scarce, a library's role is still unambiguous. In some countries where access to information is now akin to access to electricity or water, the reason to have freestanding storehouses of a subset of all information is harder to articulate. Libraries in such countries can provide access to more information than any user could want or need. Ranganathan's rule "For every reader, his or her book," might be now redefined as "for every reader, huge amounts of free-floating content, anywhere, anytime."

The library itself has long been a metaphor for order and rationality. The process of searching for information within a library is done within highly structured systems and information is exposed and knowledge gained as a result of successfully navigating these preexisting structures. Because this is a complicated process, the librarian helps guide and navigate a system where every piece of content has a preordained place.

Contrast this world with the anarchy of the Web. The Web is free-associating, unrestricted and disorderly. Searching is secondary to finding and the process by which things are found is unimportant. "Collections" are temporary and subjective where a blog entry may be as valuable to the individual as an "unpublished" paper as are six pages of a book made available by Amazon. The individual searches alone without expert help and, not knowing what is undiscovered, is satisfied.

The two worlds appear to be incompatible. One represents order, one chaos. The challenge is great for organizations occupying the interstice between these two worlds. Let us call the interstice "the twilight zone."

Rod Serling used the term "twilight zone" in the 1950s and 60s to refer to his fictional TV world where things were not as they seemed and strange things happened to ordinary people. And indeed, many information professionals think strange things are happening in their world.

But twilight itself is not inherently strange. The term refers to the light in the sky between full night and sunrise, or the light in the sky between sunset and full night. Light is low and the world seems indistinct. What is familiar in full light loses clarity and is ill-defined. However, the world in all its messy, complicated, rich detail is still there. It is just the lack of light being beamed to human eyeballs that makes the landscape of the perceivable world ill-defined and difficult to navigate.

As we make our way through the twilight zone, we seek familiar objects, shapes and routes, relying on what we know to guide us. We must look not for the details that are hard to see, but instead seek to discern patterns in the environment that will help us determine where we are and where we should go.

This report seeks to discern patterns in the twilight zone and to serve as a tour guide through the landscape that chaos and order inhabit together. The tour stops at major attractions, overlooking many minor ones not because they are uninteresting but because there are so many. The report is divided into five landscape sections. All are highly interconnected and trends in one section show up in others, viewed through a different lens—a different twist of the kaleidoscope that makes a new pattern. The final section attempts to identify the main patterns in the landscape and suggest some implications of this effort at pattern recognition.

"We have no future because our present is too volatile. We have only risk management. The spinning of the given moment's scenarios."

William Gibson[4]

4. William Gibson, *Pattern Recognition* (New York: G.P. Putnam's Sons, 2003).

Purpose, Scope & Notes on Methodology

Purpose

The purpose of *The 2003 OCLC Environmental Scan: Pattern Recognition* is the identification and description of issues and trends that are impacting and will impact OCLC, libraries, museums, archives and other allied organizations, positively and negatively.

Scope

The scope of the environmental scan is the social, political, economic and technological spheres in which OCLC, libraries, museums, archives and allied organizations operate.

The geographic scope of the report is, as much as possible, international. Little is published or available (either formally or informally) on many of the trend areas covered in this report for countries in transition but interesting areas for future investigation are evident.

Any one of the topics covered in this report could comprise a separate report of its own but this document is not intended to be exhaustive or comprehensive or even a "stand-alone" report. It is a high-level view of the landscape, sufficient to inform, stimulate discussion and serve as an outline of where more in-depth research of trends and issues is deemed desirable and necessary by OCLC and by OCLC members.

The report represents the synthesis of a great deal of information. To keep this report to a manageable, readable length, trend information is presented in two main ways. The narrative follows the same structure throughout the five "Landscape" sections: major trends are identified and then discussed. Charts, graphs and illustrations have been used throughout as a way to present information that might otherwise take many words to communicate. And, finally, readers will see patterns emerge among the trends, viewed through the lens of each of the landscapes.

Methods and research

Interviews and focus groups

OCLC staff conducted interviews with 100 librarians, vendors, archivists and other people operating in the information world. OCLC staff also conducted focus groups with senior citizens, teachers and high school students.

The interviews substantially inform many of the trends identified in this Scan. These people had interesting things to say about the general state of the profession, opportunities, funding challenges, teenagers and much more. Throughout the report you will see paraphrases from our interviewees printed in the margins. These are not quotes; they are paraphrases of what was said, as recorded by the OCLC interviewer. And because of this, they are also unattributed paraphrases except to note what sectors of the information community the interviewees represent.

Methodology

Much of the research for the report was done without using traditional, library-based, abstracting and indexing services, except to verify bibliographic data.[1]

Using the Google search engine, it was easy to find what used to be called "gray literature"—statistical data, conference presentations and proceedings—material that used to be quite difficult to identify and locate in a pre-Web world. It is still not easy to find such material using many traditional library catalogs and resources. This difficulty is something you might reflect on as you read the report.

Countries included in the Environmental Scan

A worldwide lens was used to construct this scan. Detailed education, library and technology spend data was collected for a subset of countries. This subset was constructed based on data availability and geographic representation. The sample size chosen represents approximately 60 percent of the world's population and 85 percent of the world's gross domestic product. The following countries comprise the sample:

Australia	Germany	Norway	Trinidad & Tobago
Brazil	Hungary	Saudi Arabia	Uganda
Canada	India	Singapore	United Arab Emirates (U.A.E.)
Chile	Italy	Slovenia	United Kingdom
China	Japan	South Africa	United States
Colombia	Malaysia	South Korea	
Croatia	Mexico	Spain	
France	Netherlands	Sri Lanka	

---

1. And as verification is a time-consuming task requiring patience and persistence, recognition must be made of the many hours spent by staff of the OCLC Information Center on this work.

The Social Landscape

We're Coming Unwired

The freeways are humming with wireless WAPping,
And thrumming with fingers incessantly tapping
On palmtops and laptops and cellular keys,
As we drive with our midbrains and steer with our knees.

The joe in the Jag is composing an e-mail
To explain why he's late to a furious female,
Whom he'll presently placate by pointing his Palm
To get two dozen roses from Flowers.com.

There's an M&A gal in a 528
Who is dotting the i's on a deal that will mate
The nation of Greece with a content provider,
As she's merging herself, with the center divider.

Every Jack in his Jeep, every Jill in her Hyundai,
Is communing like mad with the *Spiritus Mundi:*
They are holding their phones in their teeth while they punch in
The name of the joint they're reserving for luncheon;
They get quotes from Lord Byron, or Chemdex and Chiron,
Oblivious all to the sound of the siren;
They are checking their flights,
As they whiz through red lights,
While an oncoming semi is flashing its brights ...
If you're holding some Nokia or 3Com, I'd park it.
I've a feeling success has been killing their market.

Geoffrey Nunberg[1]
April 17, 2000

1.   www-csli.stanford.edu/~nunberg/poetastery.html.

Percentage of the population who are Internet users by country

- 50.0 – 70.0%
- 40.0 – 49.9%
- 30.0 – 39.9%
- 20.0 – 29.9%
- 10.0 – 19.9%
- < 10%

Internet usage

Country	% Population using the Internet	Country	% Population using the Internet	Country	% Population using the Internet
Norway	59.7%	Singapore	33.7%	Croatia	5.7%
United States	50.9%	Slovenia	31.0%	Brazil	4.5%
South Korea	50.5%	Malaysia	28.7%	Mexico	3.5%
Netherlands	49.2%	Italy	28.4%	Colombia	2.8%
Japan	44.0%	France	26.2%	China	2.6%
Canada	42.3%	Chile	20.0%	Saudi Arabia	1.3%
United Kingdom	40.1%	Spain	18.4%	Sri Lanka	0.8%
U.A.E.	39.9%	Hungary	14.7%	India	0.7%
Australia	38.8%	Trinidad & Tobago	10.3%	Uganda	0.2%
Germany	37.0%	South Africa	7.0%		

Sources: World Development Indicators Database, World Bank (July 2003).

The environmental scan begins with the "information consumer."[2] Without this person, there would be no libraries and no need for OCLC. But, the relationship between the librarian and the information seeker has often been uneasy—at least from the librarian's viewpoint.

Librarian yearns to see more of Information Consumer who is apathetic or indifferent to the wishes of Librarian. Librarian tries to be more accommodating by renovating the Home Page to be more attractive to Information Consumer who finds the changes pleasant enough. But while Librarian was busy sprucing up the Home Page—moving things from here to there and recovering the worn upholstery—Information Consumer has been hanging out at the Information Mall. Now Information Consumer is critical of what seems to be old-fashioned, fussy—and boring—decorating at the Home Page. Librarian tells Information Consumer that the Information Mall is shallow and disorganized and that anything found there is possibly shoddy and not to be trusted. Information Consumer isn't listening. Information Consumer is perfectly happy at the Information Mall.

Major trends

Three major trends have been selected to show information consumer characteristics.

- **Self-service: moving to self-sufficiency**
- **Satisfaction**
- **Seamlessness**

Self-service: moving to self-sufficiency

Users DO know what they're doing!
Industry Pundit

Banking, shopping, entertainment, research, travel, job seeking, chatting—pick a category and one theme will ring clear—self-service. People of all age groups are spending more time online doing things for themselves. According to one study, 71.1 percent of Americans were using the Internet in 2002; of these, 51.9 percent of them were reading news online and 35.5 percent were seeking medical information. Perhaps not coincidentally, 34 percent of Internet users in 2002 were older than 65, belying the stereotype of the youthful Web surfer.[3] Internet use is not only a U.S. phenomenon; many sources show significant Internet usage worldwide.[4]

In less than half a decade, consumers worldwide have learned to become efficient online purchasers. Studies show that many of the early roadblocks of online exchange—slow access, poor customer service, lack of security—have largely been eliminated. Almost half of the U.S. population purchased books online in 2002.[5]

The growth rates for using online services in the U.S. have also been experienced by the major economies worldwide. More than 30 percent of

---

2. The term is used both in the sense of one who purchases and ingests.
3. Jeffrey I. Cole, *The UCLA Internet Report: Surveying the Digital Future.* Year Three, 18, 21.
4. The CIA Factbook 2003.
5. Cole, *UCLA Internet Report,* 42.

consumers across the U.S., Europe and China now bank[6] online and in France more than 40 percent of online shoppers have purchased travel services over the Web.[7] Online banking and online travel activities have disintermediated the humans who used to be the gatekeepers and guides to these services, but self-sufficiency and convenience are prime drivers for the consumer.

Online content[9] purchases continue to be strong. According to a report issued by the Online Publishers Association, U.S. consumer spending on online content exceeded $1.3 billion in 2002. Some 14.2 million U.S. consumers paid for online content last year, up 43 percent. Yahoo was the leading U.S. destination for consumer content purchases, followed by Match.com—a dominance reflecting the large amounts of content aggregated by the top revenue generators. Annual subscriptions, interestingly, are the dominant pricing model, accounting for 41 percent of online content sales. The average price for monthly subscriptions online was $10.32.[10] In a similar report also issued in 2003, Jupiter Research found paid content revenues in Western Europe to be 361 million Euros in 2002, projecting a rise to 2.366 billion Euros by 2007.[11]

The significance of all this activity taking place on the Internet is that, worldwide, the trend is an increasing comfort with Web-based information and content sources. The information consumer operates in an increasingly autonomous way, interacting not with institutions but with operations and activities: one does "online banking" not "goes to the bank." Can't remember what the address of your virtual bank is? No problem. "Google"[12] it.

Google is not the only search engine. It isn't the only one people use. But it is by far the most commonly used one. On September 7, 2003, Google turned five. It answers 200 million search requests a day in 88 languages.[13] The information consumer searches Google to find old girlfriends, cars, scholarly papers presented at conferences, jokes about librarians, a quotation by William Gibson, the number of searches done on Google, e-mail addresses, the time in Helsinki and an image of Monet's *Waterlilies*. And the odds are that the information consumer considers these searches successful.

"The arrival of Google five years ago served as a kind of upgrade for the entire Web. Searching for information went from a sluggish, unreliable process to something you could do with genuine confidence. If it was online somewhere, Google and its ingenious PageRank system would find what you were looking for—and more often than not, the information would arrive in Google's top 10 results."[15]

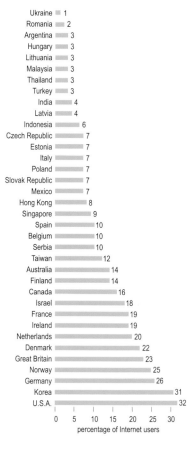

Percent of internet users who have bought goods and services online during the past month—June, 2002[8]

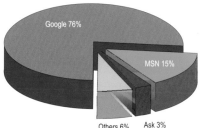

Web searching technology[14]

6. More than one-third (37 percent) of all European Internet users, a total of 60 million people, performed banking transactions online in 2002. The number is projected to increase to 130 million by 2007. Forrester Research as reported in "Metrics," *CIO Magazine* (March 25, 2003).

7. The TNS Interactive-Global eCommerce Report 2002, E-mail address: interactive@tns-global.com.

8. Ibid.

9. "Content" discussed in this paragraph does not include books. It includes business, research, greeting cards, games, newspapers, horoscopes, digital music, adult entertainment, directories, credit information and sports, for example.

10. *Online Paid Content U.S. Market Spending Report, Q4 & FY2002,* Online Publishers Association (March 2003), www.online-publishers.org/opa_paid_content_report_030403.pdf.

11. As reported in a CyberAtlas report on paid content, http://cyberatlas.internet.com/markets/retailing/print/0,,6061_2189551,00.html (April 11, 2003).

12. The term is used as described at www.wordspy.com/words/google.asp. Google™ is a trademark identifying the search technology and services of Google Technologies Inc.

13. Jefferson Graham, "The Search Engine That Could," *USA Today* (August 26, 2003), www.usatoday.com/tech/news/2003-08-25-google_x.htm.

14. Danny Sullivan, searchenginewatch.com (provided by numbers from comScore Media Metrix) (August 1, 2003).

15. Steven Johnson, "Digging for Googleholes: Google may be our new god, but it's not omnipotent," *Slate* (posted Wednesday, July 16, 2003), http://slate.msn.com/id/2085668.

Satisfaction

Surveys confirm that information consumers are pleased with the results of their online activities.

Several recent studies indicate that information consumers are, by and large, satisfied with the quality of the information they find on the Web. During 2002, Outsell studied over 30,000 U.S. Internet information seekers. More than 78 percent of survey respondents said the open Web is providing "most of what they need."[16] Well over half of those surveyed responded "Nothing is missing." In 2002, the *UCLA Internet Report* found that 52.8 percent of users surveyed believed that most or all of the information is reliable and accurate and 39.9 percent thought about half of the information was reliable and accurate.[17]

The growing demand for information online has spawned the explosion of Internet-accessible "ask-a services." Worldwide, 193,000 Internet sites use the phrase "Ask a Librarian." What isn't known is how many users of such

Sample Ask-A Services*

Directories
AskA+ Locator (part of the Virtual Reference Desk)
refdesk.com

General
Abuzz
AskBAR
Ask an Expert
Allexperts.com
Ask the Old Buzzard
Ask Jeeves
Ask Madge
Ask PointAsk

Ask Zack
CNN.com: Ask CNN
Electronic Emissary
Experts.com
Google Answers
Imagiverse
Internet Public Library
Keen.com
Wondir

Legal
Ask the Specialist
Ask-A-Lawyer

Math and Science
Ask-A-Geologist
Ask Dr. Math
Ask Dr. Universe
Ask a Mad Scientist
Ask Shamu
Ask A Space Scientist
How Things Work
Science Canada
Scientific American: Ask the Expert
SpaceKids: Ask Experts

Medical/Health
Ask Jack!
FindCancerExperts.com
Go Ask Alice!
Mdexpert.com

Art and Humanities
Ask Joan of Art
Ask the Oracle
Library of Congress: American Memory

Family and Personal
Ask Madge
iVillage — Experts Directory ("dozens of experts")

College and University Admissions
About College
iVillage: Ask the College Advisor

Linguistics and Urbanism
grammarNOW!
Handwriting Help for Kids
Slavic Reference Service

*Compiled by OCLC Information Center Staff.

16. Interview with Leigh Watson Healey of Outsell, Inc., (July 2003).
17. Cole, *UCLA Internet Report,* 18.

services have access to similar library services, and why nonlibrary-based reference services might be chosen over a library's service. What is clear is that information seekers are willing to pay for the convenience of online information services.

Information professionals are, generally, skeptical about the quality of answers provided through "ask-a services," the sources that are used to answer questions and the resources suggested for further investigations. However, a recent study conducted by Cornell librarians to compare and contrast the Cornell digital reference services with Google Answers yielded some very interesting results and raises some provocative questions about the use of highly trained, relatively expensive information professionals to answer simple reference questions.[18]

Librarians also wonder why individuals would pay for answers to questions when answers were available for free at their local libraries. Consumers are willing to pay for convenience.[19] But for the many people who do not yet have access to virtual reference services, the information hunt would mean a physical visit to the library. And while the answers may not come with a bill, there are costs associated with this.

There are features and services built into most Web sites that allow the information consumer to share. Instead of asking the librarian to use ILL to move an item from one library to another, the Web-savvy consumer can poke the ubiquitous "e-mail this article" button and off the content goes to you and several friends. In a work environment, it's a lot faster to send articles of interest this way to colleagues than it is to print an e-journal article and distribute it. And it may be that the e-mailed article might not be a scholarly article but expediency overrules effort. Call this IUE: Inter User Exchange.

Librarians worry that information found using search engines does not have the credibility and authority of information found in libraries, and that people will not learn basic information seeking skills. They worry that due to inadequate search terms and skills, much valuable material may be undiscovered.

There are some points to be made about these worries. First, most library users do not make a stop at the reference desk as they embark on their information safari with a well-trained guide. They boldly set off to look for answers on their own. This may take the form of wandering around the stacks, browsing and waiting for serendipity to strike. Or they make use of

What does a visit to a U.S. public library cost?			
Estimates	Minutes	$50,000 Annual income	$85,000 Annual income
Travel time	20	$ 8.00	$13.60
Time in library	30	$12.00	$20.40
Return travel time	20	$ 8.00	$13.60
Per capita library expenditures[1]	----	$ 6.43	$ 6.43
TOTAL		$26.43	$40.43

1. *Public Libraries in the United States:* Fiscal Year 2001, U.S. Dept. of Education. NCES 2003-399.

What does a visit to a U.S. doctor cost?			
Estimates	Minutes	$50,000 Annual income	$85,000 Annual income
Travel time	20	$ 8.00	$ 13.60
Wait time[1]	19	$ 7.60	$ 12.90
Time with doctor[2]	15	$ 6.00	$ 10.20
Return travel time	20	$ 8.00	$ 13.60
Charge/Fee[3]	----	$60.00	$ 60.00
TOTAL		$89.60	$110.30

1. "The Waiting (and Waiting and Waiting) Room," OnHealth.com, Patients' Rights Column (August 27, 1999).
2. Tracey Walker, "Medical Visits Get Group Mentality Approach," *Managed Healthcare* 10 (October 2000): 10.
3. Ray Carter, "Lower Reimbursement Rates Lead to More Cost-shifting," *Journal Record*, Oklahoma City, OK (July 30, 2003). (See Google Answer below.)

E-mail to a friend

Google Answers

In preparation of this chart, we submitted our question to Google Answers.

"What is the average cost of a visit to the doctor?"

We received an answer in 41 minutes.

Although we did not consider the source provided to be the most authoritative, the Google Answer matched our cited source.

18. Anne R. Kenney and others, "Google Meets eBay," *D-Lib Magazine* 9, no.6 (June 2003).
19. Jessamyn West, "Google Answers is Not the Answer," *American Libraries* 34, no.6 (June/July 2003): 55.

the filtering services the library provides: the online catalog and indexes. It is very likely that the terms being used in the catalog and the indexes are not the "best" ones—the ones a librarian would suggest—but unless each information seeker has a guardian librarian perched on a shoulder, the "good enough" terms will usually suffice. And the library user will never know what was missed.

Library collections contain material representing the gamut of opinions on topics. Any large academic or public library might own material on parapsychology, on Holocaust denial, on euthanasia, on the chemical processes for making LSD. There is nothing inherent in the organization and structure of the library that marks this content as "possibly illegal, fraudulent or outright crazy—use at your own risk." And librarians will vociferously defend the individual's right of access to such materials. But what this means, of course, is that many users of libraries also find material of dubious authority, quality, accuracy and reliability.

The indisputable fact is that information and content on the open Web is far easier and convenient to access and find than is information and content in libraries, virtual or physical. The downside is that there is no controlled vocabulary and no classification system to bring the intellectual order of a library to the Web. The upside is that there is no controlled vocabulary and no classification system. The information consumer types a term into a box, clicks a button and sees results immediately. For the most part the information consumer is satisfied. As any marketer knows, it is very difficult to get satisfied consumers to change brands. There has to be a very clear payoff and advantage.

Seamlessness

The traditional separation of academic, leisure and work time is fusing into a seamless world aided and supported by nomadic computing and information appliances that support multiple activities. This phenomenon is most marked among young adults,[20] but one only has to look at advertisements in any business magazines or newspapers to find images of people sitting on beaches, in restaurants and other leisure locations, making critical business decisions or sales, using some kind of wireless appliance. And the advent of wireless appliances and communication is allowing less developed countries a chance to leapfrog a generation of landlocked technology.

But it is young adults that this section focuses on: they are the most numerous population on a college campus, and they form a significant portion of any public library's community of users. It is also with this group that the biggest disconnect between the current structure and presentation of content in libraries is most evident. The Internet is a technology as ordinary as television to this group and the Web is an information necessity.

There's an adage that goes like this: Technology is what happened after you were born.

The library community is mostly in denial about real issues and questions.

Industry Pundit

Instead of wringing our hands over students using the Web for research, we should help them learn to use Web materials and resources more effectively.

Director, Academic Library

---

20. Among 18- to 24-year-olds in the United States, **12 percent** rely solely on wireless phones for communication, and that number is expected to increase by **28 percent** over the next five years. Yankee Group as reported in *CIO Magazine* (August 19, 2003).

The freshman class of 2003 grew up with computers, multimedia, the Internet and a wired world. Twenty percent of them began using computers between the ages of 5 and 8. By the time they were 16–18 **all** of them had begun using computers.[21] Their world is a seamless "infosphere" where the boundaries between work, play and study are gone. Computers are not technology and multitasking is a way of life. This generation of young adults mixes work and social activities, and the lines between workplace and home are blurred. The compartmentalization of leisure activities from work activities that their parents still mostly adhere to is largely unknown to the current group of college students. "Today's digital kids think of information and communications technology (ICT) as something akin to oxygen: they expect it, it's what they breathe and it's how they live. They use ICT to meet, play, date and learn. It's an integral part of their social life; it's how they acknowledge each other and form their personal identities. Furthermore, ICT to some degree has been supporting their learning activities since their first Web search and surf years ago."[22]

A significant indicator of the collaborative, synchronous world that lies alongside the asynchronous one adults inhabit is the amount of "gaming" among students as reported by a recently released Pew report.[23] Sixty-five percent of college students surveyed reported playing video, computer or online games regularly or occasionally. This gaming activity is not segmented into a part of the day deemed "leisure." Students report playing games in class, while visiting friends, while instant messaging and in between doing schoolwork. They do this using any convenient computer. The report concludes that students are taking their leisure "in sips, rather than gulps" and suggests that not enough research is being done on what this "always on" interactive and seamless world implies for the future of work and entertainment. "The rate at which information is assimilated into knowledge and knowledge is synthesized into new forms [...] is vastly more multidimensional than the 19th century paradigm of classroom instruction."[24]

Contrast this seamless world with what students experience at most libraries. Despite the increase in "information commons" in academic libraries and banks of publicly available computers in public libraries, libraries frequently designate different computers for access to content as they do for e-mail and writing papers. And even if this is not the case, there are almost always separate spheres of information presented: "Web resources," "article databases," "online catalog." And once inside these spheres, the

> *There's a seamlessness to the interactions of young people. Their academic, social and community lives are merged. But library environments still cater to our generation with separate spheres of information. We have to figure out how to be relevant.*
>
> Director, Public Library

> *Interactivity is a hallmark of young people's lives. They live in a collaborative world that doesn't exist for adults.*
>
> Director, Public Library

21. Steve Jones et al., *The Internet Goes to College: How Students are Living in the Future with Today's Technology* (Washington, D.C.: Pew Internet & American Life Project, 2002), 2. www.pewinternet.org/reports/pdfs/PIP_College_Report.pdf.

22. John Seely Brown, "Learning in the Digital Age," In *The Internet and the University: 2001 Forum,* edited by Maureen Devlin, Richard Larson and Joel Meyerson, 65–91 (Boulder, CO: EDUCAUSE, 2002): 70.

23. Steve Jones et al., *Let the Games Begin: Gaming Technology and Entertainment Among College Students* (Washington, D.C.: Pew Internet & American Life Project, 2003), www.pewinternet.org/reports/pdfs/PIP_College_Gaming_Reporta.pdf.

24. J.C. Herz, "Gaming the System: What Higher Education Can Learn from Multiplayer Online Worlds," In *The Internet and the University: 2001 Forum.* edited by Maureen Devlin, Richard Larson and Joel Meyerson, 169–191 (Boulder, CO: EDUCAUSE, 2002): 173, www.educause.edu/ir/library/pdf/ffpiu019.pdf.

information seeker is often presented with brand names: Newsbank, ProQuest, WebCat. Given the characteristics of young adults suggested above, it is perhaps not surprising that Pew reports 73 percent of college students said they use the Internet more than the library.[25]

"Librarians are put in the unfortunate position of telling people to eat their spinach, that fast food searching isn't enough. But if a vendor could deliver quality material through Google interfaces, they would have an advantage."[26]

The Anatomy of a Gamer

Profile:

Male, age 20
College Student, University of Toronto
Asian Studies major

Learning Style:

Socially contextual learning and peer-to-peer learning

Affiliations:

Soccer club
Founding member of the Gaming Club, University of Toronto

"We are a group of individuals who enjoy strategy games. The club exists to provide a forum for us to get together and indulge in such pastimes as Dungeons & Dragons, Magic: The Gathering and Diplomacy. We encourage any interested people to come out and join us."

(Source: This club description is on the student affairs site at the University of Toronto, July 2003.)

Favorite pastimes:

Biking
Music
"Gaming the System"

For years, computer games flourished in academic computer labs. Ironically, although they were never sanctioned activities, games provide a social nexus for undergraduates and graduate students to cluster and explore difficult issues or situations.

As computers moved out of the lab and into the living room, budding programmers dedicated their time (and sometimes dropped out of school) to create games for a burgeoning class of enthusiasts. Their products were fly-by-night programs, built quickly and shared freely. When the Internet became available in the early 1990s their already robust bulletin boards, magazines and modem culture migrated onto the Net. After Id Software opened the source code of Doom level editors in 1994, player modifications exploded and the gaming phenomena was born. By the end of the millennium, nearly every strategy game and combat game on the market had a built-in editor and tools to create custom characters or scenarios. Driven by the human desire to compete and collaborate, and a dynamic, distributed ecosystem of official games sites, the gaming industry flourished.

Today, some 65 percent of college students report being regular or occasional game players (Pew study). Better tools, faster machines and better collaboration are driving new levels of involvement. If a gamer doesn't understand something, a continuously updated, distributed knowledge base maintained by a sprawling community of players is available to learn from. "Newbies" are taught by more skilled and experienced players. Far from being every man for himself, multiplayer online games actively foster the formation of teams, clans, guilds and other self-organizing groups. The construction capabilities built into games allow players to stretch their experiences in new and unexpected directions to extend the value of the game. The rate at which information is assimilated into knowledge and knowledge is synthesized into new forms is vastly more multidimensional than the 19th century paradigm of classroom instruction.

Herz, J.C. "Gaming the System: What Higher Education Can Learn from Multiplayer Online Worlds." In *The Internet and the University: 2001 Forum.* Edited by Maureen Devlin, Richard Larson and Joel Meyerson, 169-191 (Boulder, CO: EDUCAUSE, 2002). www.educause.edu/ir/library/pdf/ffpiu019.pdf
J.C. Herz's e-mail is jc@joysticknation.com.

---

25. Steve Jones et al., *The Internet Goes to College,* 12.
26. Rich Wiggins quoted in Barbara Quint, "ProQuest Introduces PQNext Interface," *Newsbreaks & the Weekly News Digest* (August 4, 2003), www.infotoday.com/newsbreaks/nb030804-2.shtml.

The strong interest in more collaborative, seamless environments has not gone unnoticed by information sector companies. Many large software and content providers are building integrated platforms and suites of software to allow for the exchange of information, enable commerce and support new and dynamic forms of collaboration. One-to-one, one-to-many and many-to-many exchange mechanisms are becoming embedded in the general communication devices and software that consumers use. Amazon, Google and Yahoo are actively embedding these new collaborative technologies in the services.

Libraries are not using many of these collaborative technologies.

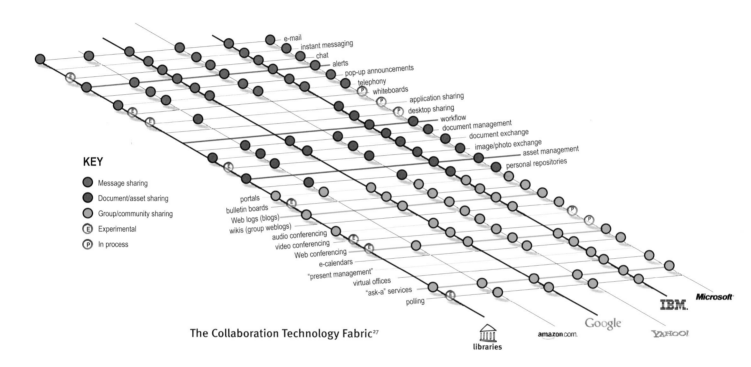

KEY

- ● Message sharing
- ● Document/asset sharing
- ○ Group/community sharing
- Ⓔ Experimental
- Ⓟ In process

The Collaboration Technology Fabric[27]

In the old days the library was it—there weren't many other choices. Today, that is not the case.

Director, OCLC Regional Service Provider

Self-sufficiency, satisfaction, seamlessness

In late October 2003, without much corporate fanfare, Amazon released a "search inside" feature that allows full-text searching of about one quarter of a million e-versions of print books. This is about as many titles as a physical bookstore has, and a great deal less than many libraries own. Amazon is the first commercial entity to offer full-text searching at no cost (although it requires searchers be registered Amazon customers). At bottom, the feature is meant to help Amazon sell more books, something Amazon is quite up-front about. But, the significance of Amazon's full-text search feature is not so much about the cool technology behind the feature, or about content. The significance is about self-sufficiency, satisfaction and seamlessness. In other words, the "Aha!" factor is not about technology; it's about what can be done *with* the technology. Stephan Levy of *Newsweek* wrote: "It's a lightning bolt from the future. Some people literally broke out in tears as they punched in queries and unearthed obscure but relevant citations."[28]

Predictably, this feature was met with negative and positive reactions. On the negative side, people worried that only big publishers would be able to participate, further alienating small and niche publishers, or that searchers would pirate copy, or that the information consumer would now use Amazon for research in lieu of libraries' much larger collections. On the positive side, people heralded this move as a way to rejuvenate access to and use of out-of-print material, as a powerful adjunct to research, and as a new way to link readers with their interests. Karen Schneider, well-known among librarians, wrote on her blog, *Free Range Librarian:* "I heard repeated reference from presenters and keynoters [at the Internet Librarian conference] to the significance of Amazon's new Search Inside the Book feature, confirming my own gut reaction that this is big, really big, in ways we don't yet understand or appreciate."[29]

Newsweek's Levy captures one of the ways in which this is big: "The ability to record events was a transforming development for our entire species. But until very recently—until the Web—the vast collective documentary created by humans has always been limited because the works we created were so difficult to access."[30] Book titles can never capture the nature of the content in books, and even good subject cataloging is limited to providing broad brush strokes about content. But titles and subject headings do not help people differentiate among similar sounding books. And this is where full-text searching can expose useful and relevant content that is invisible using title and subject searches. As librarians know, the more specific the term, the more likely a full-text search will be successful. So, searching for "amazon" in Amazon returns almost 14,000 book titles and excerpts on the river, the company, female warriors and the children's book *Swallows and Amazons*. Searching for "Boadicea" returns 434 titles, including *Personal History* by Katharine Graham of *The Washington Post* fame. She relates on page 15 that her mother was asked by the sculptor Rodin to pose for a statue of Boadicea. Who knew? "That's why the advances of Google and Amazon are so profoundly important. They are harbingers of a new kind of history, where

Every Jack in his Jeep, every Jill in her Hyundai, Is communing like mad with the Spiritus Mundi:

Geoffrey Nunberg

28. Stephan Levy, "Welcome to History 2.0," *Newsweek,* (November 10, 2003): 58.
29. Karen Schneider, *Free Range Librarian,* (November 9, 2003), http://frl.bluehighways.com/frlarchives/000097.html.
30. Levy, "Welcome to History 2.0."

the world's information is not only more plentiful and diverse, but astonishingly accessible."[31] Won't it be nice when an advance in the library community is so well-covered and greeted with such warmth?

"[A] seamless customer experience across channels will often require internal enterprise priorities, processes and management responsibilities to be redesigned, which may be just as difficult to implement as the technology aspects."[32]

The information consumer is ready.

Implications

- Seamlessness is an information consumer expectation. *How could libraries be redesigned to provide a "seamless customer experience"? How could information service providers themselves provide a seamless customer experience?*

- Users will continue to use the Web and search engines to find and retrieve content and information. *Should library content and metadata be exposed in general Web search results?*

- The current virtual library and library-based content is not most searchers' first stop. *How can libraries and information service providers enter users' spaces instead of making them come to our spaces?*

- Subject boundaries are increasingly self-defined, on-the-fly. *How do we keep the benefits of metadata and classification while making them invisible?*

31. Ibid.
32. J.Fenn, "Self-Service From 2003-2013," *Research Note,* SPA-18-9637 (Stamford, CT: Gartner, Inc,. December 3, 2002): 1.

The Economic Landscape

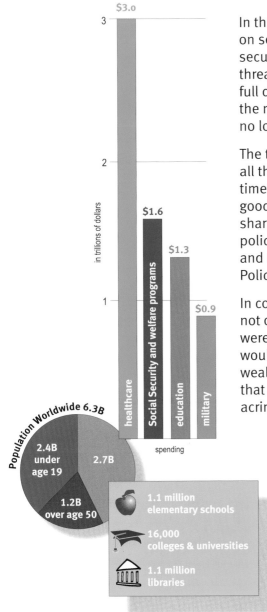

in trillions of dollars

- $3.0 healthcare
- $1.6 Social Security and welfare programs
- $1.3 education
- $0.9 military

spending

Population Worldwide 6.3B
- 2.4B under age 19
- 2.7B
- 1.2B over age 50

1.1 million elementary schools

16,000 colleges & universities

1.1 million libraries

The public and public goods[1]

In these early years of the 21st century, many countries face growing demands on services funded centrally. Surging healthcare costs, increasing national security programs, increasing education costs and aging populations threaten to outstrip the capacity or willingness of communities to meet the full cost of such services through taxation. Add slowing global economies to the mix and the challenges of funding the ever-growing needs of citizens are no longer merely academic.

The trends that we highlight revolve around a cycle of not enough money for all the programs democratic and open societies fund. In good economic times, funding the "public good" is painless, as there is money for all such goods. When those funds decline, for whatever reasons, public scrutiny sharpens toward expenditures on such nonrevenue producing sectors as police, fire, sewers, roads, libraries, schools and so on. Communities, large and small, are then pushed to declare where scarce funds will be expended. Police or sewers? Roads or libraries?

In countries in transition these issues are more clear-cut. The question is not one of dismantling existing abundant social services and goods. If there were a Maslow's Hierarchy of Community Needs, a stable electricity system would be funded before schools are equipped with swimming pools. But for wealthier countries unused to making such choices, one overarching trend is that scarce funds for supporting all the public goods will make for an acrimonious process of resource allocation.

Major trends

- Slow economic growth worldwide
- Worldwide education and library spending
- A silver lining—shared infrastructures
- Funding the public good

1. Please see "Sources" on pp. 147–48 for the complete list of sources consulted.

Gross domestic product (GDP) by country

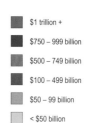

- $1 trillion +
- $750 – 999 billion
- $500 – 749 billion
- $100 – 499 billion
- $50 – 99 billion
- < $50 billion

Country GDP

Country	World Rank	GDP Billion	Country	World Rank	GDP Billion	Country	World Rank	GDP Billion
United States	1	$ 10,417	Brazil	13	$ 452	Croatia	63	$ 22
Japan	2	$ 3,979	Netherlands	14	$ 414	Slovenia	67	$ 21
Germany	3	$ 1,976	Australia	15	$ 411	Sri Lanka	73	$ 16
United Kingdom	4	$ 1,552	Norway	21	$ 189	Trinidad & Tobago	88	$ 9
France	5	$ 1,410	Saudi Arabia	23	$ 186	Uganda	105	$ 6
China	6	$ 1,237	South Africa	35	$ 104			
Italy	7	$ 1,181	Malaysia	37	$ 95			
Canada	8	$ 716	Singapore	40	$ 87			
Spain	9	$ 650	Colombia	41	$ 82			
Mexico	10	$ 637	U.A.E.	43	$ 71			
India	11	$ 515	Hungary	45	$ 66			
South Korea	12	$ 477	Chile	46	$ 64			

Source: World Development Indicators Database, World Bank (July 2003).

Slow economic growth worldwide

Economic contraction is forcing service reductions

"More than a million Americans will lose publicly-funded healthcare. Crime-wracked Oakland, California, where the number of murders nearly doubled last year, is cutting millions from its police budget. Massachusetts won't pay for dentures, eyeglasses or prosthetics for low-income residents anymore. Oregon public schoolchildren will likely attend 15 fewer days of classes. Ohio and Kentucky are closing prisons. Illinois is slashing childcare funds for welfare families by half. The Fire Department of New York, formerly the heroes of 9/11 but now just another costly line item in the city's shrinking budget, is set to cut eight engine companies and reduce staffing on the remaining units from five firefighters to four."[2]

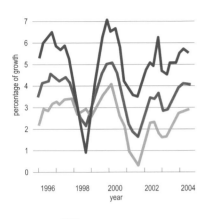

KEY
- ■ Emerging markets
- ■ The world
- ■ Industrial countries

GDP growth rate of world economies[3]

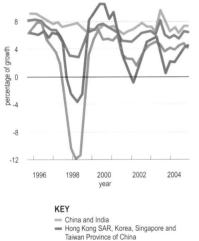

KEY
- ■ China and India
- ■ Hong Kong SAR, Korea, Singapore and Taiwan Province of China
- ■ Emerging Asia
- ■ Indonesia, Malaysia, the Philippines and Thailand

GDP growth rate of Asian economies[3]

The worldwide economy is slowly recovering from a turbulent economic start to the 21st century. The worldwide gross domestic product (GDP) growth rate for advanced economies sank to less than one percent in 2001, and has struggled through 2002 and 2003.[3] During 2002, North America experienced an abrupt end to more than 18 years of economic growth. This period of radical economic shifts has left governments and public service organizations in the difficult position of having to rely on program cuts or painful tax increases to balance budgets when expected revenue predictions proved to be unreliable. In the United States, the effects of these sudden shifts have been traumatic. State governments are in the process of closing deficits for fiscal year 2003 that total nearly $80 billion. Budget deficits for fiscal year 2004 are estimated to exceed $70 billion. Most U.S. economists expect state fiscal problems to continue in fiscal year 2005, and further rounds of tax increases and program cuts will likely be made as states struggle to meet their balanced budget requirements.[4]

The worldwide outlook is slightly better, but the 2003 International Monetary Fund (IMF) predictions show slow economic growth. Estimated worldwide GDP is expected to grow 3.2 percent in 2004, with slower growth expected in the United States (2.6 percent) and Europe (0.5 percent). Developing economies are the bright spot, with GDP estimated to grow at 5.0 percent.

While long-range economic outlooks show recovering growth worldwide, there is little evidence that governments in industralized countries are likely to see substantial revenue increases to reverse the funding cuts required during the past two years. Worldwide unemployment rates are expected to remain at high levels through 2004. Worldwide equity markets are still approximately 50 percent below their early 2000 peak levels.

These ongoing fiscal constraints have contributed to a tendency for communities—local, regional and national—to reexamine the traditional practice by democratic societies of automatically funding "the public good."

We will return to the discussion of future funding for public goods, but we begin this section with a review of global education and library spending and a closer look at the traditional sources and uses of libraries funding, both in the U.S. and for selected regions across the globe where data is available.

2. *Salon* [online magazine] (January 22, 2003).
3. International Monetary Fund, *World Economic Outlook: Growth and Institutions* (September, 2003).
4. Elizabeth McNichol, *Using Income Taxes to Address State Budget Shortfalls,* Center on Budget and Policy Priorities (June 13, 2003), www.centeronbudget.org/2-11-03sfp.htm.

Worldwide education and library spending

In 2001, the 29 countries covered in this report spent approximately $1.1 trillion dollars on education or roughly 4.1 percent of their collective gross domestic product. The United States spent the most on education in 2001 at roughly $500 billion, followed by Japan, Germany and France at $139 billion, $89 billion and $82 billion respectively. While the U.S. spent the most in absolute dollars, it ranked tenth in education spending as a percent of GDP at 4.8 percent. Saudi Arabia ranked first, investing 9.5 percent of GDP in education. The top five include Norway, Malaysia, France and South Africa. All five countries spent in excess of 5 percent of GDP on education. The United Arab Emirates came in 29th at 1.9 percent of GDP.

Education spending per capita provides another lens to view worldwide education spending. Norway leads the group again with an estimated $2,850 per capita spent on education. The United States ranks second at approximately $1,780. The top five also include France, The Netherlands and Canada. Each spent more than $1,200 in education per capita in 2001. Uganda ranked 29th at approximately $5 per capita.[5]

Library spending for the selected countries totaled approximately $29 billion in 2000. This represents roughly 94 percent of the estimated worldwide annual library expenditure of $31 billion. It is important to note that this total figure is approximate. Several of the sample countries (including Brazil, Colombia, Saudi Arabia and China) do not report, or regularly collect, library expenditures.[6]

The United States led 2000 library spending at approximately $12 billion, with Japan ($3.2B), the United Kingdom ($3.2B),

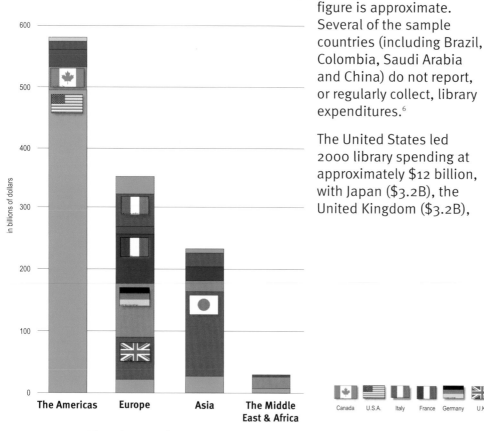

Education spending by region

5. UNESCO Institute for Statistics (May 2003).
6 LibEcon.org: *A Research Study in International Library Economics*, Institute of Public Finance, United Kingdom, www.libecon.org/default.asp. Data used were the 2000 gross estimates.

Italy ($1.6B) and France ($1.6B) rounding out the top five sample countries. The United States represents approximately 40 percent of sample country library spending and the top five countries represent 75 percent of total estimated library expenditures.

A look at library spending as a percent of country GDP again provides a different view. South Korea led the field at 0.31 percent of GDP, followed by the United Kingdom (0.21 percent), Australia (0.20 percent) and Canada (0.20 percent). The United States ranked eighth at 0.12 percent.

Examining annual library spending per capita provides a similar top five list. The United Kingdom tops the field at approximately $54 per capita. Canada ($45), Australia ($45), the United States ($43) and Norway ($40) create a familiar leading group. There is a wide degree of disparity across the group with relatively high GDP countries like Spain and Mexico ranking low on library spending per capita. As expected, high-population countries (with the exception of the United States and Japan) ranked relatively low on library spending per capita.[7]

A comparison of country education expenditure and country library expenditure does not provide any obvious associations. While it holds that most of the countries that rank in the top ten for education spending also rank in the top ten for library spending, there are obvious exceptions. Spain, Mexico and China rank high in education spending, but did not rank in the

Five countries—the United States, Japan, the United Kingdom, Italy and France— represent nearly 75 percent of the total estimated worldwide library spending.

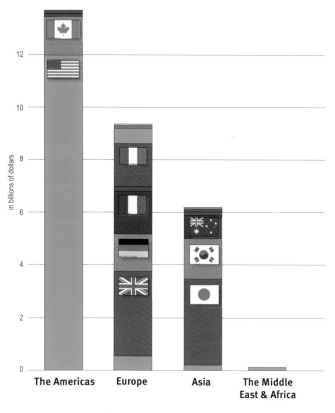

Library spending by region

7. Ibid.

top ten for library spending, based on available data. Saudi Arabia ranked first in total educational spending per GDP, but based on available estimates, trails the sample countries in library spending. It is important to note again that there is no worldwide library expenditures reporting standard. Some library spending could be included in country total educational expenditures, which will skew a comparative view. Interestingly, anecdotal information suggests that one challenge for many countries is corruption. Funds earmarked for public entities—libraries included—may be diverted long before they reach their intended recipients.[8]

Trend data could provide very useful information, giving insights into regions where investments in libraries are growing or contracting. Retrospective trend information is not currently available for worldwide library expenditures. Several of the library expenditure sources used to compile this report are now collecting data for 2003, which will provide management trend information for the future.

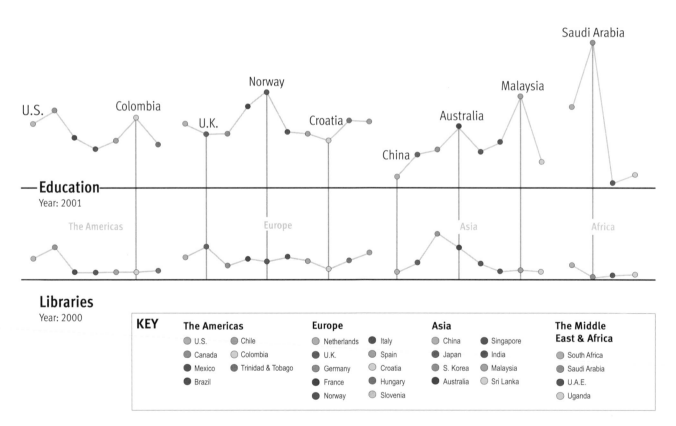

GDP spending on education and libraries[9]

8. Interview with Bob Usherwood, University of Sheffield and principal investigator of the IFLA sponsored study, *Public Library Politics—an International Perspective.*
9. World Development Indicators Database, World Bank (July 2003).

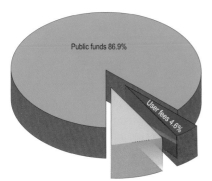

Public funds 86.9%

User fees 4.6%

Other (grants, donations) 8.5%

Sources of library funds

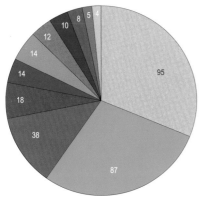

Total funding 2000– 2002
($, millions)

KEY

- Bill & Melinda Gates Foundation
- Mellon Foundation
- Lilly Endowment Inc.
- Carnegie Corporation of New York
- Duke Endowment
- Ford Foundation
- Pew Charitable Trusts
- Champlin Foundation
- Kresge Foundation
- Rockefeller Foundation
- Ahmanson Foundation

**Largest private library
funding foundations**

Library funds—sources

Funding source information was available for the year 2000 for 15 of the 29 sample countries selected for this scan.[10] For the 15 countries covered, library funding came from three primary sources: public funding, user fees and charges and "other." Public funds are defined as funds received from central or local governments; user fees and charges are income generated by library operations and from fees, charges and subscriptions. "Other" includes miscellaneous sources such as donations, grants, proceeds from asset sales and interest earned.

For all countries covered, public funding is the primary source of library funding, comprising 87 percent of funding on average. Norway and France received more than 90 percent of their funding from public sources in 2000. United States public libraries receive 87 percent of their funding from public sources. User fees and charges represent 4 percent of library funding on average, with the remainder of resources coming from the miscellaneous "other" sources. The amount of funding from nonpublic sources varies significantly across the sample, with Hungary receiving over 20 percent of its funding from "other" sources. The United States receives approximately 8 percent of its funding from these miscellaneous sources.

U.S. funding—foundation and private grants

Although worldwide data was not available to analyze the primary sources of nonpublic funding around the world, data does exist that can provide an overview of the nonpublic funding in the United States.

Foundations and private grant funding are significant sources of U.S. library funding. Based on figures presented by the Foundation Center, the nation's leading authority on philanthropy, U.S. library grant funding averages approximately $200–300 million annually, based on the Center's report of grants over $10,000 from the top 1,200 granting institutions. 2000 and 2001 were particularly strong years, totaling nearly $300 million annually.[11] The spike in 2000 and 2001 is attributed to large donations from the Bill & Melinda Gates Foundation.

Foundation Center: U.S. grants for libraries worldwide 2000–2002 ($, millions)[11]					
Year	Number of grants	Total grant funding	% funding from Gates*	Number of grants outside U.S.	Grant funding outside U.S.
2000	1,542	$352	19%	78	$30
2001	2,220	$283	10%	94	$24
2002	468	$100	0%	52	$12
Three-year total	4,230	$735	13%	224	$66
* Percent of total reported grant funding awarded to libraries by the Bill & Melinda Gates Foundation.					

10 LibEcon.org: Research Study.

11. Foundation Center, *Grant$ for Libraries and Information Services*, New York, N.Y. (2000), http://fconline.fdncenter.org/dt_files/search_grants.html.

In 2000, $30 million was granted to organizations outside of the U.S. Of this amount, $13 million were Gates Foundation grants, with Canada receiving $5.5 million and Chile receiving $7.5 million. In 2001, the $24 million granted outside the U.S. included $6 million to Austria, $5 million to England and nearly $4 million to South Africa.

In 2002, grants totaling $12 million were awarded to libraries outside of the U.S., including those in Mexico, South Africa, Latvia and Kenya.

Historically, the Andrew W. Mellon Foundation has been the largest single private foundation source of grants for libraries. While the Gates Foundation led in 2000 and 2001, Mellon has consistently supported libraries as a part of its overall mission in support of scholarship. It ranks as one of the top ten private granting organizations in the world. Together these top ten agencies have provided libraries more than $210 million in grant support since 2000.

The top private granting organizations award funds for a wide variety of projects that include technology support, collections and acquisitions, programs and program development, conferences and seminars, staff, staff development, income development, campaigns, technical assistance, publications, fellowships, land acquisition and building and renovation, as well as general support, continuing support and even debt reduction.

In 2002, approximately $18 million in private grants reported to the Foundation Center were awarded for electronic media and online services.[12] Many organizations clearly benefited from Gates funding in 2000 and 2001.

The [funding agency] has no special brief for libraries as such but supports library activities as a means towards wider scholarly ends.

Director, Funding Agency

Year	Number of grants	Total grant funding	Gates* funding	Mellon funding
Electronic media & online services 2000–2002 ($, millions)[12]				
2000	117	$ 56	$ 40	$ 8
2001	808	$ 41	$ 22	$ 7
2002	52	$ 18	$ -	$ 11
Three-year total	977	$115	$ 62	$ 26

* Grant funding awarded to libraries by the Bill & Melinda Gates Foundation.

12. Foundation Center, *Grant$ for Libraries and Information Services.*

U.S. funding—government

We looked at two United States federal government organizations, the National Science Foundation (NSF) and the Institute of Museum and Library Services (IMLS) as sources of funding for libraries. The NSF is an independent agency of the U.S. government whose mission is to promote the progress of science, primarily through the initiation and support of science research programs. IMLS is a federal grant-making agency that administers the Library Services and Technology Act and the Museum Services Act.

As of August 2003, NSF had $380 million invested in ongoing projects that include the descriptor term "library." Of nearly 500 ongoing NSF-supported projects reviewed for this scan, only three were actually granted to *libraries*[13]. While NSF grants often fund research on organization, storage and dissemination of information, grants are not typically awarded to the institution's information center or library. Also, NSF customarily provides grants to researchers, not libraries.

IMLS grant support consists of the disbursement of the federal Library Services and Technology Act (LSTA) funds. Over 80 percent of the funding provided to libraries by IMLS is granted directly to the states for further disbursement. Of direct grants to states, IMLS awarded $30 million net in grant monies during FY2003. In this same fiscal year, funding for leadership grants nearly doubled to more than 15 percent at the expense of conservation, general operating support and museum assessment.

LSTA funds available to libraries are expected to increase from the current level of $180 million. In September 2003, The Museum and Library Services Act of 2003 was signed into law, providing appropriations authority of $232 million annually for libraries for FY 2004 through 2009.[14] For 2004, IMLS requested nearly a 16 percent budget increase. These requests were modified in a late November 2003 appropriations conference and votes on these appropriations are still pending. The amounts expected to pass represent an 11 percent increase in total, including a 5.4 percent increase for state grants and a doubling of "21st Century Librarian" recruiting funds from $10 to $20 million.[15,16]

Senator Judd Gregg, Chairman Senate Committee on Health, Education, Labor and Pensions says: "Even with the rise of 24-hour news cycle and Internet blog sites, there will always be the need for a good book. This bill helps to ensure our libraries do not become a relic of the past, but remain an important part of our neighborhoods and our culture… as well as allow[s] funds to be used to recruit new professionals into the field of library science."[17]

IMLS Office of Library Program Funds Funding FY2003 (in millions)	
Grants to state agencies	$150.4
Leadership grants for libraries	11.0
21st Century Librarians	9.9
General operations support	5.7
Native American grants	3.1
Total grants	$180.1

www.imls.gov/whatsnew/leg/finalfy2003.htm

Special collections will be funded by grants and donations. Libraries will be strapped and it is likely that we will have to go after private dollars to fund these initiatives.

Director, Academic Library

13. National Science Foundation, NSF Awards, www.fastlane.nsf.gov/a6/A6SrchAwdf.htm. One was the Library of Congress, one was for a consortium and one for a library at a science conservatory.

14. Institute of Museum and Library Services, "President Signs Bill Reauthorizing Museum and Library Services Act" (September 23, 2003), www.imls.gov/whatsnew/current/092503.htm.

15. American Library Association, ALAWON, "Conference Agreement Library Funding Numbers." www.ala.org/Content/NavigationMenu/Our_Association/Offices/ALA_Washington/News2/20034/101dec02.htm#1.

16. Danielle Dowling, Congressional Affairs Specialist, IMLS (interview December 2003).

17. Institute of Museum and Library Services, "Statements From Congress On Passage Of Museum And Library Act," Senator Judd Gregg, Chairman Senate Committee on Health, Education, Labor and Pensions, www.imls.gov/whatsnew/current/092503b.htm.

Library funds—uses[18]

Resource allocation patterns among library funds across the countries covered in this report showed striking similarities, despite major disparities in other areas. On average, the countries included in the scan spent 53 percent of annual operating funds on staff, 27 percent on print material stock, 3 percent on electronic content and annual electronic subscriptions and 17 percent on other, primarily facilities and administration. Members of the Academic Research Libraries group in the United States show interesting simularities.

Staffing allocation was similar across most countries and regions in the sample. The majority of countries in the sample allocated between 52 percent and 60 percent of their resources to staff. Germany allocated the highest percentage to staff at approximately 60 percent; Mexico was the lowest at 42 percent. It is interesting that automation-poor countries show similar staffing expenditures to automation-rich countries. Where, then, are productivity gains that generally follow increased automation?

There is wide variability in the percentage of library funds allocated to electronic content and annual electronic subscriptions. Spain reported allocation of less than one tenth of one percent of its operating funds to electronic resources. The United Kingdom spent close to 8 percent on electronic resources in 2000. The Netherlands reported approximately 5 percent and the United States spent approximately 2 percent.

Considering the amount of ink devoted to "the shift from print to electronic" in the library literature, the low percentages of materials funds devoted to electronic resources seems disproportionate to the hype.

As funding to libraries contracts or remains static (while the cost of materials does not), staffing and materials budgets receive increased scrutiny from funding agencies and library administrators. It is clear that libraries must find cost reduction opportunities in both of these budget categories.

Although there is no worldwide data available to analyze cost reallocation patterns, there is information available for U.S. libraries. Cost reductions in materials budgets, especially print materials, are evident across all library sizes and types. Libraries are changing both the amount and format of materials purchased. *Library Journal's* annual buying survey of public libraries indicates libraries are buying fewer materials, cutting standing orders and buying lower-cost materials, choosing paperback over hardback, for example. In the interviews OCLC did for this report, several public librarians reported they were ordering bestsellers in paperback to accommodate the need for multiple copies at the cheapest cost. They also reported significantly reducing other types of print purchases in favor of DVDs and CDs—media their constituents request. Reductions in print reference materials were identified as the "hardest hit" areas in the 2003 *Library Journal* survey, with 57 percent of public libraries indicating that they will reduce spending on these materials.

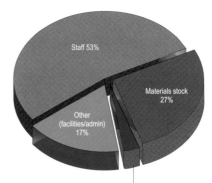

Uses of library funds worldwide

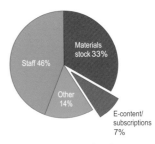

Use of library funds— ARL University libraries 2001–02

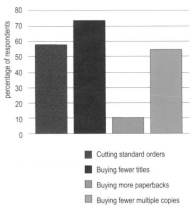

Source: 2003 Library Journal Buying Survey

U.S. public libraries—materials budget response to budget cuts

---

18. Please see "Sources" on pp. 147–48 for the complete list of sources consulted.

> *The State Library is facing a 79% cut in the acquisitions budget this fiscal year. Print items are the first to go. It's kind of a grim time.*
>
> **State Librarian**

A silver lining—shared infrastructures

Budget reductions create both challenges and opportunities.

The need to reduce staff costs, the need to lower materials costs while at the same time preserving these assets, the need to address the unfunded liability of capital renewal, and the increasing expectations of the technology-empowered user will have significant impacts on library services.

Some librarians interviewed for this report indicated that budget constraints could have a positive, liberating impact on libraries as it would force decisions avoided in more comfortable times. "It will allow us to make the shifts we know we have needed to make for some time" was a common way of expressing this.

Libraries of all types find there is increasing scrutiny of the return on investment (ROI) of library services and collections—and not just from the funding agency. An increased interest among the general population in how scarce tax dollars are spent has brought attention to what libraries and publicly-funded museums spend tax dollars on. As one public library director told the OCLC interviewer: a good library board insists that the library pass muster in the court of public opinion and this means a lot of public scrutiny and involvement.

> *Libraries are in the business of saving the [parent] institution money by providing rational management of vital information resources on which the institution depends.*
>
> **Associate University Librarian**

One of the most interesting patterns emerging on the horizon is a renewed look at the power (and ROI) of shared library systems and infrastructures. In the United States, consortia are (re)forming and states are coming together to look anew at the feasibility of utilizing shared technology infrastructures. Slow or negative economic growth compels publicly-funded institutions to be very, very clear in articulating the economic value to the community at large. The higher education sector and the government have done this for years by tracking the ROI of a college education to society at large. The value of a college degree can be expressed as value returned to society in economic terms.

The library and its sister organizations—museums, archives and historical societies—have not, in any organized fashion, used similar tactics in documenting the economic good of their continued healthy existence. Most people believe libraries represent a fundamental public good in a democracy; however, without a clearly articulated demonstration of value, taxpayers may choose not to fund this particular public good. "Sherrill Wilson would rather see Buncombe County close its libraries than raise property taxes."[19]

> *Libraries may have to stop thinking about their collections as their primary asset.*
>
> **Industry Pundit**

"Information is free." The commodity that forms the basis of a library's commerce is often thought by its constituents to be without cost when it is delivered across the network. Jim Gray, a Microsoft researcher, articulated the issues clearly in a March 2003 report.[20] The "cost of providing computing" is absolutely not free. Here are some highlights from that report:

> **"Computing is free."** The world's most powerful computer is free (SETI@Home is a 54 teraflops machine). Google freely provides a trillion searches per year

19. www.citizen-times.com/ Quote not archived (June 23, 2002).
20. Jim Gray, *Distributed Computing Economics,* Technical Report, MSR-TR-2003-24 (Redmond WA: Microsoft Research, March 2003).

to the world's largest online database (2 petabytes). Hotmail freely carries a trillion e-mail messages per year. Amazon.com offers a free book search tool. Many sites offer free news and other free content. Movies, sports events, concerts and entertainment are freely available via television.[21]

Actually, it's not free, but most computing is now so inexpensive that advertising can pay for it. The content is not really free; it is paid for by advertising. Advertisers routinely pay more than a dollar per thousand impressions (CPM). If Google or Hotmail can collect a dollar per CPM, the resulting billion dollars per year will more than pay for their development and operating expenses. If they can deliver a search or a mail message for a few micro-dollars, the advertising pays them a few milli-dollars for the incidental "eyeballs." So, these services are not free—advertising pays for them.

Computing costs hundreds of billions of dollars per year: IBM, HP, Dell, Unisys, NEC and Sun each sell billions of dollars of computers each year. Software companies like Microsoft, IBM, Oracle and Computer Associates sell billions of dollars of software per year. So, computing is obviously not free.

Total Cost of Ownership (TCO) is more than a trillion dollars per year. Operations costs far exceed capital costs. Hardware and software are minor parts of the total cost of ownership. Hardware comprises less than half the total cost; some claim less than 10 percent of the cost of a computing service. So, the real cost of computing is measured in trillions of dollars per year.

Megaservices like Yahoo!, Google and Hotmail have relatively low operations and staff costs. These megaservices have discovered ways to deliver content for less than advertising will fund. For example, in 2002 Google had an operations staff of 25 who managed its 2 petabyte (2^{15} bytes) database and 10,000 servers spread across several sites. Hotmail and Yahoo! cite similar numbers—small staffs manage ~300 TB of storage and more than 10,000 servers.

Outsourcing is seen as a way for smaller services to benefit from megaservice efficiencies. The outsourcing business evolved from service bureaus through timesharing and is now having a renaissance. The premise is that an outsourcing megaservice can offer routine services much more efficiently than an in-house service. Today, companies routinely outsource applications like payroll, insurance, Web presence and e-mail. Outsourcing works when it is a service business where computing is central to operating an application and supporting the customer—a high-tech, low-touch business. It is difficult to achieve economies-of-scale unless the application is nearly identical across most companies—like payroll or e-mail.[22]

An 80-percent variable cost structure in a technology-intensive field, where common procedures and practices are shared across institutions, provides opportunity for cost reduction.

JSTOR, a nonprofit organization founded in 1995 to help the scholarly community take advantage of advances in information technologies, has built a model that demonstrates the operating cost advantages of leveraging shared technology infrastructures to store electronic journals. In a 2001

Operations costs far exceed capital costs. Hardware and software are minor parts of the total cost of ownership.
Microsoft Technology Report, March 2003[21]

Universities are increasingly called to demonstrate their ROI, and libraries will be increasingly held accountable. They need to be better at showing the value of long-term investment in the information infrastructure. When a road is built, the ROI isn't in the transportation department—it's in the community at large.
Director, National Licensing Project

---

21. This paper makes broad statements about the economics of computing. The numbers are fluid—costs change every day. They are approximate to within a factor of 3. For this specific fact: SETI@Home averaged 54 teraflops (floating point operations per second) on 1/26/2003, handily beating the sum of the combined peak performance of the top four of the TOP500 supercomputers registered at www.top500.org/ on that day.

22 Jim Gray, *Distributed Computing Economics.*

We've had incredible cuts—40 percent of staff and funding. We need to convince the administration and the public that if they want this stuff around we need more support.

Director, State Historical Society

Educause Review article, JSTOR reported an estimated annual cost of access advantage of more than 60 percent by moving from a traditional, open-stack journal management system to a centrally-administered electronic content system.[23]

A 1999 study by AT&T Labs suggests that for every dollar libraries spend to purchase an article, they spend twice as much on ordering, cataloging, shelving, circulating and providing reference assistance.[24] The economic return possible by reducing these shared operating costs across just a fraction of the world's million libraries is substantial.

Driving efficiencies and looking for innovative ways to share technical infrastructures is certainly not new for libraries. WorldCat, a shared infrastructure application, jointly created by libraries, was launched in 1971. Since 1978, the Dutch shared cataloguing system, Gemeenschappelijk Geautomatiseerd Catalogiseersysteem (GGC), has helped libraries across The Netherlands leverage shared solutions. Many other shared applications are providing libraries worldwide with substantial cost savings. But increasing financial constraints and the growing array of nonlibrary information services are driving libraries to come together to collaborate in new ways. Working together to create common efficiencies and improved ROI for stakeholders will change libraries' economics. It is required. For what's at stake is the adequate funding of the public good.

My library's reputation is predicated on what it owns. How will it maintain that reputation as it moves to digital? A new model needs to be developed.

Director, Academic Library

Funding the public good

"We've been hearing from people, 'Don't raise our property taxes. Don't raise our property taxes,' said Alderman Mike D'Amato, a member of the Library Board of Austin, Texas, which earlier this month cast a unanimous vote to close its Villard Avenue branch, the least busy of the city's 12 neighborhood libraries. 'Do you want your taxes cut?' D'Amato asked. 'Do you want your services the same? Because it's impossible to do both.'"[25]

There has been a worldwide shift in the past 15 years or so from public to private support for and provision of goods and services. This can be seen in a wide variety of sectors, such as telecommunications, railroads, hospitals, public radio, gas and electricity utilities and higher education. Increasingly, costs are moved to the consumer.

It is interesting to study the varied approaches to the funding of public programs in emerging economies where historical approaches are either not available to use as guides or are simply no longer adequate to match surging community needs. The following look at the funding of public libraries in the world's fastest growing economy, China, highlights the variety of solutions that can emerge when citizens, commercial enterprises and governments collaborate and compete for public programs.

23. Kevin M. Guthrie, "Archiving in the Digital Age There's a Will, But is There a Way?" *EDUCAUSE Review* (November/December 2001).
24. Andrew Odlyzko, "Competition and cooperation: Libraries and publishers in the transition to electronic scholarly journals," AT&T Labs—Research, Revised Version (April 27, 1999).
25. Mike Clark-Madison, "The Budget Battles, Round 3," *The Austin Chronicle* [online] 22, No. 52 (August 29–September 4, 2003): n.p.

Funding the public good in China

Libraries as cultural centers in large, new communities in Guangzhou, China

Huang Qunqing and Zhang Xuhuang
The Science and Technology Library of Guangdong Province
People's Republic of China

Guangzhou (population 10 million) is the capital city of South China's Guangdong Province and has been developing rapidly in recent years. Its GDP grew 12 percent in 2002. Residents' incomes are increasing and people are investing in cars and new homes. Many large new housing estates have been built in rural areas of the

province around Guangzhou. Real estate developers are adding many interesting new amenities to their developments in efforts to attract buyers such as regular bus service to the city, recreation facilities and community libraries.

A survey of ten large, new country housing estates conducted by Huang Qunqing and Zhang Xuhuang of The Science and Technology Library of Guangdong Province found that each development had, or had plans to construct, a community library. Ranging in size from small facilities of approximately 100m^2 to three-story facilities, each library surveyed had unique operating and funding strategies.

One of the largest community libraries, the Guangzhou Country Garden Library, is a 685m^2 facility located on the top floor of the estate's clubhouse. Built in 1999, the Guangzhou Estate Company invested 10,000 RMB to purchase the initial collection of 12,000 books, 90 magazine

Guangzhou

Guangdong Province

China—profile of a growth economy[26]

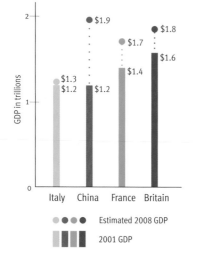

China—GDP estimated growth[26]

- Estimated 2008 GDP
- 2001 GDP

China's annual GDP growth was 7.9 percent from 1995–2002, making it one of the world's fastest growing economies. The chart above shows China's estimated GDP for 2008 in relation to three other industrial countries.

China—manufacturing center[27]

World's leading producer of these goods:

1990	2002	
• Cotton textiles	• Cotton textiles	• Desktop PCs
• Televisions	• Televisions	• DVD players
	• Refrigerators	• Bicycles
	• Cameras	• Motorbikes
	• Cell phones	

In 2002, China became the first country in more than 20 years to attract more foreign investment than the United States.[27]

China $53.2B

United States $52.7B

subscriptions and 40 newspapers. The estate company maintains an operating account, financed by a resident's realty management fee, to replenish books and fund librarians' salaries. The library is free for residents of the community.

Opened jointly by the estate company and the Guangzhou municipal library, the Riverside Garden Library is a free library that not only serves residents but also farmers and other citizens in the neighboring communities. The real estate company and the municipal library jointly manage the library. The Guangzhou library established and maintains the book collection and provides professional training. The real estate company is responsible for the facility, staff and the replenishment of magazines and newspapers.

Other models include the library in Guangdi Garden, which opened as a bookstore. Residents can purchase a

reading card for 50 CNY that gives them the right to read or buy the library/bookstore books. The library is run on contract with the bookstore owner who must agree to provide abundant free browsing and reading materials.

Several estate companies have entered into cooperative arrangements with schools to build branch libraries in their housing estates. Finally, other communities have chosen to operate local libraries that are stocked, staffed and maintained by the residents.

The entrepreneurial nature of recent real estate development in China has been good for the proliferation of libraries, but the financial sustainability of many of these new real estate-financed libraries is in question over the long run. Many estate clubhouse programs are running at operating deficits that may make it difficult to continue to sustain the current level of library investment. The library is a

public good, not a commercial business, so it may be hard for developers to maintain funding.

Residents of these new estates recognize that libraries and cultural facilities are desirable features of their communities, but ones that will require funding in excess of estate management fees. There is an increasing push among residents for local government support of libraries and other public services.

[Excerpted and edited from a paper presented at the World Library and Information Congress: 69th IFLA General Conference and Council, August 2003].

China—education and technology[26]

China's population is 1.3 billion (July 2003 est.)[28]

China graduated 2 million technicians and engineers in 2003.[27]

In 2001, 110 out of every 1,000 people in China owned a mobile phone.[26]

In China, there are 4 to 6 million new cell phone subscribers every six months.[27]

Chinese spending on education

| Estimated 2008 education spending (2.2% GDP) | $43B |
| 2001 education spending (2.2% GDP) | $27B |

If China continues to fund education at 2.2 percent of GDP, by 2008 Chinese economic expansion will fund a 50-percent growth in education spending.[26]

26. Development Data Group, World Bank (October 2003).
27. K. Lieberthal and G. Lieberthal, "The Great Transition," *The Harvard Business Review* (October 2003): 71–80.
28. CIA, The World Factbook 2003, www.cia.gov/cia/publications/factbook/index.html.

Along with a general shift to privatization of public services in the developed countries, there has been an increasing emphasis on assessment and accountability—although these are hardly new societal expectations.

John Cotton Dana, a key figure in 20th century librarianship, wrote in 1920:

"All public institutions…should give returns for their cost; and those returns should be in good degree positive, definite, visible and measurable […] Common sense demands that a publicly-supported institution do something for its supporters and that some part at least of what it does be capable of clear description and downright valuation."[29]

What was true in 1920 still holds today. Accessment and accountability, then, are not new themes. To measure accountability, libraries have traditionally focused on their collections—the size, the variety, the utility as measured by circulation.

In a world where cuts in materials budgets are commonplace and where content is not scarce, trends suggest that "clear description and downright valuation" of libraries must place them squarely and unambiguously in the larger network of learning resources that includes museums, public broadcasting and community organizations that are part of a knowledge-based society.

Robert S. Martin, the Director of the Institute of Museum and Library Services writes:

"Libraries of all types provide a broad range of resources and services for the communities they serve. They preserve our rich and diverse culture and history and transmit it from one generation to the next. They provide economic development. They provide extraordinary opportunities for recreation and enjoyment. And they serve as a primary social agency for education, providing resources and services that both support and complement agencies of formal education."[30]

The challenge, then, is how to continue to adequately fund the public good.

29. John Cotton Dana, *The New Museum: Selected Writings by John Cotton Dana*, edited by William Penniston (1999). Quoted in Robert S. Martin, "Reaching Across Library Boundaries," In *Emerging Visions for Access in the 21st Century Library*, 3–16, Council on Library and Information Resources and the California Digital Library, (Washington DC: CLIR, August 2003): 10.
30. Robert S. Martin, "Reaching Across Library Boundaries," In *Emerging Visions for Access in the 21st Century Library*, 3–16, Council on Library and Information Resources and the California Digital Library (Washington DC: CLIR, August 2003): 11.

Implications

- Public funding for libraries and allied organizations will likely continue to decline or remain at low levels for several years. *What can we do to shift internal resources to maintain and increase services in the face of static or declining funding?*

- Not enough is known about models of library funding globally. There may be lessons to learn for North American libraries. *How do other countries fund libraries and allied organizations, and what might work?*

- 75 percent of the world's library spending is concentrated in 5 countries. *How can these countries help build global communities in partnership with countries where public funding of libraries is relatively low?*

- Productivity gains from technology adoption and innovation is not as apparent in libraries as in other industries. *How can technology be leveraged to serve more people and deliver more services*?

- Libraries and allied organizations cannot assume public funding will always be available. *What can be done to demonstrate (and increase) the economic value of libraries?*

Technology Landscape

Embedded Connectivity
(smart, dynamic)

Connectivity Era

Logical Connectivity
(wireless/service oriented, semantic, event-based)

Physical Connectivity
(networked, group productivity information overload)

Personal Computing
(individual productivity tools)

Computing Era

Mainframe Computing
(organizational, department productivity)

| 1970 | 1980 | 1990 | 2000 | 2010 | 2020 | 2030 |

Gartner, Inc. research[1]

Major trends

- **Bringing structure to unstructured data**
- **Distributed, component-based software**
- **A move to open-source software**
- **Security, authentication and Digital Rights Management**

The patterns[2] surfacing in the technology and information architecture landscape suggest we are headed into a period of technology change that may be as significant as the shift from mainframe architectures to client/server architectures in the 1980s. Whereas PCs and client/server software made it possible to distribute both applications and data closer to their users in the 1980s, the next-generation technology architecture will distribute even smaller units of software over the Internet directly to distant users as well as directly to devices and objects such as equipment on the factory floor, packages on store shelves or servers and hardware devices in a partner organization. Using sophisticated messaging, open-source solutions

1. J. Fenn and others, *CIO Update: Key Technology Predictions, 2003 to 2012*, IGG-01082003-02 (Stamford, CT: Gartner, Inc., January 8, 2003).
2. Larry Downes, "Unleashing Killer Architecture: The Shape of Things to Come," *CIO Magazine* (June 15, 2003): n.p., www.cio.com/archive/061503/architecture.html.

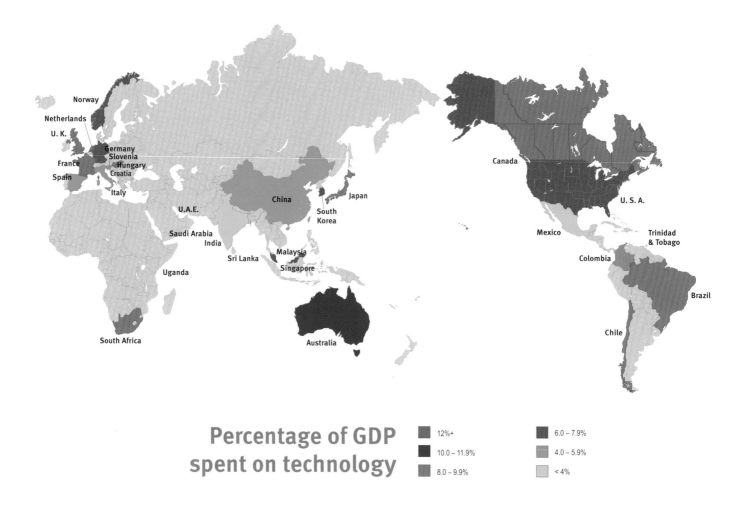

Percentage of GDP spent on technology

- 12%+
- 10.0 – 11.9%
- 8.0 – 9.9%
- 6.0 – 7.9%
- 4.0 – 5.9%
- < 4%

Country spending on information and communications technology

Country	% GDP	Country	% GDP	Country	% GDP
Colombia	12.0%	Brazil	8.3%	Slovenia	4.7%
Australia	10.7%	Chile	8.1%	India	3.9%
Singapore	9.9%	United States	7.9%	Mexico	3.2%
United Kingdom	9.7%	Germany	7.9%	Croatia	N/A
Japan	9.6%	South Korea	7.4%	Sri Lanka	N/A
Netherlands	9.3%	Norway	7.2%	Trinidad & Tobago	N/A
South Africa	9.2%	Malaysia	6.6%	U.A.E.	N/A
France	9.1%	Italy	5.7%	Uganda	N/A
Hungary	8.9%	China	5.7%	Saudi Arabia	N/A
Canada	8.7%	Spain	5.1%		

Sources: World Development Indicators Database–2003 Edition, World Bank.

and new security protocols, data processing and information exchange will become tightly connected to business processes, facilitating new kinds of collaboration, partnering and outsourcing relationships.

The individual movements that are fueling this next-generation architecture scenario have been percolating for some time. The unprecedented spread of data exchange standards like TCP/IP, XML and MP3, and broad access to nonproprietary networking and data communications infrastructure (the Internet) have supported rising technology waves and strong development undercurrents. Many experts say that the combination of new standards, distributed software and a worldwide Internet infrastructure will create a profoundly new technology architecture landscape within the next five years.

We identified the rapid adoption of collaboration technologies earlier in this document. In this section we will explore four additional aspects of this technology landscape that will likely impact information creation, dissemination and management. We will conclude by providing a framework for analyzing some of the specific applications, technologies and standards that will be the building components of this new environment.

Bringing structure to unstructured data

A scan of the technology landscape identifies increased investments in technologies and standards that allow organizations to bring structure to unstructured data.

In the interviews OCLC staff did with 100 professionals actively engaged in the creation, management and dissemination of information, there was a clearly expressed interest in technologies and methods that will allow information professionals (and end users) to bring structure to the vast amount of unstructured data that is available in today's Information Mall. Increased user interest in unstructured or uncataloged information such as historical photograph collections, audio clips, research notes, genealogy materials and other riches hidden in library special collections has ignited conversations of how best to create metadata and methods to ensure dynamic and meaningful links to and among these currently unstructured information objects.

This drive to bring structure to unstructured data is being spurred by not only the library and information community, but by the business and government communities worldwide. It is estimated that 85 percent of the content in an enterprise is unstructured content[3] and as enterprises look for new forms of competitive advantages, they are working to harness the power of this unstructured data.

Two dominant technical and structural approaches have emerged: a reliance on search technologies and a trend towards automated data categorization.

3. Interview with Outsell, Inc., Analyst Marc Strohlein (July 2003).

Search technologies

With the Web at 6 billion pages and growing, and organizational information page counts dwarfing that figure, finding what you what when you want it can be a daunting task. This problem has dominated the technology landscape in the last several years. The "killer app" solution is "search."

Searching has become an international pastime. Over 625 million searches are conducted on the top eight search engines each day.[4] Yet, even after five years of rapid growth, search engine technology is considered by many analysts to be in its early stages. The search engine arena is highly competitive, with nearly a hundred solutions on the market from companies ranging from upstarts like Endeca to the leaders Google, Yahoo! and Microsoft.

The following chart provides a brief overview of the top search technologies and sample vendors.

A survey of search technologies

Search technologies[5]	Definition	Sample vendors
Boolean (extended Boolean)	Retrieves documents based on the number of times the keywords appear in the text.	Virtually all search engines
Clustering	Dynamically creates "clusters" of documents grouped by similarity, usually based on a statistical analysis.	Autonomy, GammaSite, Vivisimo
Linguistic analysis (stemming, morphology, synonym-handling, spell-checking)	Dissects words using grammatical rules and statistics. Finds roots, alternate tenses, equivalent terms and likely misspellings.	Virtually all search engines
Natural language processing (named entity extraction, semantic analysis)	Uses grammatical rules to find and understand words in a particular category. More advanced approaches classify words by parts of speech to interpret their meaning.	Albert, Inxight Software, InQuira
Ontology (knowledge representation)	Formally describes the terms, concepts and interrelationships in a particular subject area.	Endeca, InQuira, iPhrase, Verity
Probabilistic (belief networks, inference networks, Naive Bayes)	Calculates the likelihood that the terms in a document refer to the same concept as the the query.	Autonomy, Recommind, Microsoft
Taxonomy (categorization)	Establishes the hierarchical relationships between concepts and terms in a particular search area.	GammaSite, H5 Technologies, YellowBrix
Vector-based (vector support machine)	Represents documents and queries as arrows on a multidimensional graph—and determines relevance based on their physical proximity in that space.	Convera, Google, Verity

Source: Forrester Research, Inc.

4. Danny Sullivan, *Searches Per Day,* searchenginewatch.com (February 25, 2003).
5. Chart Source: "You Are Here," by David Howard, *New Architect* (January 2003). Copyright© 2003 by CMP Media LLC, 600 Community Drive, Manhasset, NY 11030, USA. Reprinted from *NEW ARCHITECT MAGAZINE* with permission.

One 2002 estimate suggests that Google search engines handle more questions in a day and a half than all the libraries in the U.S. provide in a year.[6]

There is little doubt that the rapid adoption of search technology has dramatically increased the power and productivity of the World Wide Web. Savvy Web users have become experts at maximizing search techniques to achieve the desired output but are also beginning to demand more sophisticated (or more structured) search methodologies. A group of high school students interviewed for this scan discussed how they have learned search techniques to find the information they need for school projects.

"[Search success] depends on how to do some of your searches. Because a lot of people say when they use search engines, they don't find what they want but if you learn how to put your words in, you end up getting the results you want."[7]

Marsadie, 16-year old girl

"Yeah, with Google, you can search within your results. Like, you can type in like a general word that like, say your report is about like the Cold War. You can type in 'Cold War' and it will come up with a bunch of stuff, then you can narrow it down like you just go search within results and then type in 'Berlin Wall,' or 'Soviet Union,' or something like that...'Arms Race'...and then it will narrow it down and you can usually get better results that way."[7]

Catherine, 16-year old girl

"... I actually tried doing research on a few different things but they came up invalid or just really not good. I found better information in just a regular book."[7]

James, 17-year old boy

As users become more experienced and more discriminating, the shortcomings of current search solutions are surfacing. While many students had become very skilled at finding what they wanted, all focus group participants felt that easier search methods are needed. The experts agree. Finding known objects in huge search spaces, assembling top-down overviews that summarize the important points of a topic, and helping searchers decide what they really want when their initial search ideas are confused, misguided or ambiguous are casting doubts on the long-term viability of today's search techniques.[8]

6. Barbara Quint, "Some Advice for Google Answers," *Information Today* 19, no.6, (June 2002): 8.
7. OCLC Focus Groups, Columbus, Ohio (November 12, 2003).
8. Fred Hapgood, "Sleuthing Out Data," *CIO Magazine* (May 1, 2003), www.cio.com/archive/050103/et_article.html.

Several technology analysts surveyed for this scan said that using today's search technologies was simply "using brute force to solve the data discovery problem." Search (or search alone) is not the long-term answer for superior information discovery.

Automatic data categorization—enabling the smarter "find"

Several data organization and description technologies and methodologies are gaining popularity as ways to address the void. Data organization techniques that library science has utilized for decades are becoming popular and important outside the information management community.

"The demand, outside the library community, for information about data organization and metadata is exploding,"[9] say Gartner, Inc. technology analysts. In 2003 Gartner issued several research notes on metadata including, *Enterprises Need a Metadata Integration Strategy*[10] and *Taxonomy Creation: Bringing Order to Complexity.*[11]

Many data categorization techniques are being applied across the landscape including: taxonomies, semantics, natural-language recognition, auto-categorization, "what's related" functionality, data visualization, personalization and more. All techniques aim to help searchers find what they really want.

Data categorization is not new. "At one time, researchers speculated that solving such search problems might require artificial intelligence: systems that simulated human thought and could behave like skilled reference librarians. [...] Until recently, however, IT applications required paid humans to think up the category names, define their relationships and write the rules that channeled data into the proper boxes. As a result, the technique was limited to fields with big budgets, such as financial analysis or defense. During the past few years, however, technology development has made it much easier to automate or at least semiautomate categorization."[12] Data categorization techniques are moving from manual activities, done by librarians and other information professionals, to automated processes executed on behalf of users.

"More and more information travels with a lengthening entourage of data about itself. Autocategorization software recognizes and leverages that data."[13] Information professionals have an opportunity to leverage these new technologies to bring information management methods to a large portion of today's born-digital content.

9. Interview with Gartner, Inc., Analysts Rita Knox, Research Director and Vice President, and Debra Logan, Research Director.
10. M. Blechar, *How to Manage Your Metadata*, AV-20-5975 (Stamford, CT: Gartner, Inc., August 18, 2003).
11. M. Blechar, *Enterprises Need a Metadata Integration Strategy*, DF-20-5020 (Stamford, CT: Gartner, Inc., July 24, 2003); K. Harris and others, *Taxonomy Creation: Bringing Order to Complexity*, QA-20-8719 (Stamford, CT: Gartner, Inc., July 24, 2003).
12. Hapgood, "Sleuthing Out Data."
13. Ibid.

Distributed, component-based software

A second dominant technology architecture trend is the apparent move away from the monolithic, hard-to-maintain masses of application software code we've known in the past toward smaller components that communicate with each other to complete particular tasks.

In the future, developers and end users will license software in pieces—some from traditional application and systems software vendors and others from companies specializing in particular business functions. Open-source applications will become part of the mix. Companies will also write their own modules for activities in which they already enjoy a distinct advantage and combine them with the increasing number of standard, easily available components. These changes will help to eliminate the painful and unsatisfying make-or-buy dichotomy of today's technology environment.

In a component-based environment, information technology professionals will have the ability to manage components independently, making modifications far simpler, faster and potentially cheaper. Patrons and customers will benefit by access to information and services on more devices and at multiple, distributed points of service.

I have seen technologies come and go—and take everything with it. You can go to your Board once to ask for dollars for "big technology" but only once. I have seen many directors have to change jobs when the big bet failed.

Special Librarian

Application architecture

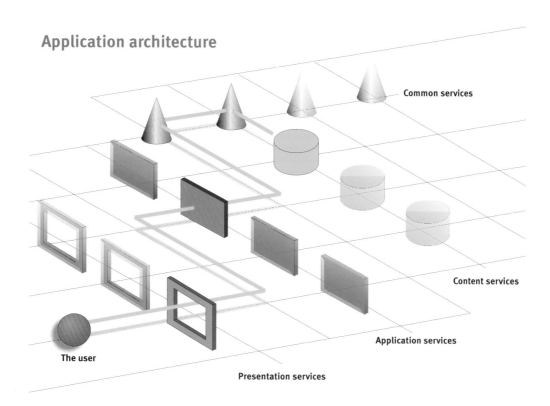

Common services

Content services

Application services

The user

Presentation services

Many technologies and standards are fueling this shift from monolithic, bound-together technology solutions to distributed, component-based software. One of the dominant enabling technologies in this arena is Web services.

Web services

Web services are commonly used business processes delivered over the Web, based on industry-wide-standards. Using Web services, small software modules located anywhere on the Web are able to interact with each other using standard protocols, making it possible to quickly link together computer systems across organizations worldwide.

Web services are receiving significant attention and funding due to the potential they hold for both users and IT departments. [14]

The chief benefits driving the interest in and adoption of Web services include:

- Web services let organizations bridge communications gaps—between software written in different programming languages, developed by different vendors, running on different operating systems.

- Web services run over the Internet, over intranets or other Internet protocol-based networks, which are common inside companies. The infrastructure required to use Web services is stable, reliable and inexpensive.

- Major technology vendors, including Hewlett-Packard, IBM, Microsoft, Oracle and Sun, have agreed to support a set of standard Web services software technologies that spell out how different computer systems should interact with each other—offering an uncommon level of cross-industry cooperation.

- Web services technologies let organizations leverage prior investments in technology. Web services are not used to build new systems from scratch but rather as tools to dynamically integrate existing computer systems to create efficiencies or deliver new capabilities.

Web services are enabling the rapid connection of information that was simply structurally impossible just a few years ago. Standards acceptance will be a critical determinant of Web services successes. The most important of these standards, XML or extensible markup language, has gained industry-wide support and acceptance.

The initial use of Web services technologies has been inside organizations. But as organizations gain experience and standards are adopted, Web services and other component-based software tools will become mainstream in the technology landscape in the next two to five years.

Leading search information provider Google is extending the reach and increasing the connectivity of its search application using Web services. It launched the Google Web APIs developer's kit in the spring of 2002. The kit,

"Originally designed to reduce costs and smoothen application integration, Web services have also become a new platform for information providers."

Elangovan Balusamy [15]

14. Sari Kalin, "The Essential Guide to Web Services," *Darwin: Business Evolving in the Information Age,* (January 2002): n.p., www.darwinmag.com.
15. Elangovan Balusamy, "Web Services Development Made Easy," Oracle Corporation (2003), http://otn.oracle.com/oramag/webcolumns/2003/techarticles/balusamy.html.

which can be downloaded over the Web, includes programming examples and a Web Services Description Language File (WSDL) for writing programs on any platform that supports Web services.

Hardware advances are also likely to reinforce Web services adoption. "Web services enable the linking of intelligence to each individual item in commerce. The Auto-ID Center at MIT estimates that about a trillion new Internet-friendly devices will be added to the network in the next 10 years. Integrating technology devices like chips and radio transmitters will simply become part of a product's basic packaging."[16]

As these technologies reach mainstream adoption, librarians and information providers must think about how to deploy Web services for their users. Many current commercial applications of Web services, from providing real-time stock quotes to information about local traffic patterns,[17] have direct corollaries to library information services.

We need to sustain the open connectivity—the linking among people, organizations, data and ideas—that drives the growth and diversity of the Web.

Industry Pundit

A move to open-source software

A move to lower cost, open-source software will enable organizations to bring solutions and services to market faster and cheaper.

When Linus Torvalds sat down in 1991 to write a version of Unix that would run on Intel chips (later to become Linux), he probably didn't think too much about creating a whole new way to develop and maintain software. Yet the

---

Top 20 projects*

FRESHMEAT

freshmeat maintains the Web's largest index of Unix and cross-platform software, themes and Palm OS software. Thousands of applications, which are preferably released under an open-source license, are meticulously cataloged in the freshmeat database, and links to new applications are added daily. www.freshmeat.net

1. **Mplayer** A movie player for Linux
2. **Linux** The Linux Kernel
3. **cdrtools** A tool to create disk-at-once and track-at-once CDs

4. **Gaim** A CTK2-based instant messaging client
5. **xine** A Unix video player
6. **MySQL Database Server** A fast SQL database server
7. **gcc** The GNU Compiler Collection
8. **TightVNC** An enhanced VNC distribution
9. **Apache** A high-performance, Unix-based HTTP server
10. **PHP** A high-level scripting language
11. **Nmap** A network exploration tool and security/port scanner
12. **phpMyAdmin** Handles the basic administration of MySQL over the WWW
13. **libcomprex GNUpdate** A compression/decompression library
14. **Webmin** A Web-based interface for Unix system administration
15. **Mozilla** A Web browser for X11

16. **GkrellM** System monitor package
17. **OpenSSL** The open-source toolkit for Secure Sockets Layer and Transport Layer Security
18. **Samba** Tools to access a server's filespace and printers via SMB
19. **libjpeg** Library of JPEG support functions
20. **LILO** Linux boot loader

* Based on number of subscriptions, URL hits and record hits as of November 29, 2003.

Source: freshmeat.net, accessed November 29, 2003.

---

16. Downes, "Unleashing Killer Architecture."
17. Balusamy, "Web Services Development."

act of opening the code to anyone interested and willing to make a contribution has had a revolutionary impact.

Fast-forward to 2001: Linux is factored into the core strategy of most major vendors (including Hewlett-Packard, IBM, Intel, Oracle and Sun Microsystems) and is increasingly the platform of choice for many server applications. Open-source development products (JBoss, FreeSQL, Tomcat) are widely available and in some cases (such as Apache) widely used. There are at least 30 Linux distributions available.

Many experts feel that although open-source applications have not yet fully matured, they believe the applications are mature enough to include as key parts of their future IT strategies.

A recent study conducted by *CIO Magazine*[18] found there is evidence the IT community is growing more comfortable with the open-source development model, reporting that open-source software will dominate as the Web server application platform and server operating system within five years. The majority (64 percent) of companies surveyed are using open source today, most frequently as a server operating system and for Web development.

CIOs surveyed say the greatest benefits from using open source are lower total cost of ownership, lower capital investment and greater reliability and uptime compared to their existing systems. IT executives report that open source provides greater flexibility and control, and faster, cheaper application development. All things being equal, the majority of IT executives surveyed said they would choose open source for a new implementation over a proprietary vendor solution.

Adoption of open-source development methods as acceptable practice is also starting to take root. The open-source development process, where volunteer developers contribute code over the Internet, does not appear to be a concern for the majority of IT executives in the *CIO Magazine* survey. When asked how comfortable their organization was with the open-source development process compared to the traditional proprietary development process (full-time, paid developers, code managed and organized centrally),

SourceFORGE.net is the largest repository of open-source code on the Internet. As of November 23, 2003, SourceForge reported hosting 71,580 projects and over 740,000 registered users. Over 1,800 open-source education projects are hosted on the site.

SourceFORGE.net

SourceFORGE: November 2003 project of the month

Creator: Tim Kosse

Age: 22

Education: Currently studying Computer Science (Dipl.) at the RWTH Aachen

Location: Aachen, Germany

Profile

Project Name: FileZilla

Founded/Started: February 2001

FileZilla, a secure FTP client for Windows, is an open-source success story. The program was started two years ago in Germany by a computer science student named Tim Kosse. While working on his degree, Tim began to write a simple FTP program for a class assignment. After the class was completed, Tim continued to improve upon the code base. Eventually he chose to host it on SourceFORGE.net. With feedback and support from the SourceFORGE.net community, Tim's code and FileZilla's feature set continued to improve. Today, the program has a thriving user base and a large community of devotees around the world. As of November 2003, the project is ranked in the top 15 projects (out of 70,000) on the site and has more than 4,000 downloads daily.*

™

* SourceFORGE.net, November 29, 2003.

18. Lorraine Cosgrove Ware, "Confidence in Open Source Growing," *CIO Research Reports* (January 7, 2003).

27 percent said they were more comfortable with open source and 36 percent said they had the same level of comfort as with the proprietary process.

Users are beginning to view many software applications as commodity products with little differentiation among vendor offerings. Open source provides organizations with another compelling choice that offers the flexibility, quality and reliability necessary to implement many functional applications to run a business. Faced with budget constraints and increased spending on security infrastructure, the open-source movement will allow organizations that cannot wait for funding to get started on IT initiatives. This will likely mean an even faster rate of new technology introductions in the future landscape.

"Amazon.com embraced open source in 2002, converting from Sun's proprietary operating system to Linux. The switch is simplifying the process by which freelance retailers known as Amazon associates can build links to Amazon applications into their Web sites, using Amazon's payment, fulfillment and customer service without actually installing the software."[19]

It is not a coincidence that many of the developers participating in the open-source arena are the same young people for whom a collaborative gaming environment is part of their social landscape.

"They care passionately that the results of their cooperative creative efforts not be appropriated, or inappropriately co-opted. That which has been achieved by sharing should, in turn, be shared with the rest of the community."[20]

Security, authentication and Digital Rights Management (DRM)

The traditional book as a thematic collection is changing. Books are being decomposed to their fundamental constituent elements.

Director, Museum Library

Moving that intellectual property around in virtual forms and formats is creating enormous challenges for authors, publishers and information providers. We don't have to look any farther than the music industry to see the dramatic changes that new access models can have on distribution of intellectual property. Sales of music via online music sites are expected to account for $1.4 billion or 11 percent of music industry sales within the next three years. By 2008, 33 percent of music industry sales will come from downloads.[21]

Three primary technology issues surfaced in our review: security, authentication and digital rights management technologies. The more we researched these topics, the more it became clear that these are not three distinct issues, but are increasingly becoming part of one highly interrelated discussion. Due to the complexity of the issues and the brevity required in

19. Downes, "Unleashing Killer Architecture."
20. Mark Federman, "Enterprise Awareness McLuhan Thinking," Keynote speech at the Information Highways Conference, Toronto, Canada (March 25, 2003): 10.
21. Forrester Research, quoted in "Online Stores Launch Flashy Campaigns to Sell That Tune," *The Wall Street Journal* (Monday, November 10, 2003).

this scan, our discussion concentrates on providing an overview of what we will define as the "secure rights management" landscape. How each individual component of secure rights management, security, authentication and Digital Rights Management (DRM) will develop independently is still very unclear. There are hundreds of players, fragmented vertical markets and fuzzy standards. What is clear is that all key players in the information supply chain—content owners, software developers, hardware vendors, wireless and network providers—and the e-commerce infrastructure and payments companies are making substantial investments in both the technology and standards of secure rights management.

At the heart of the digital rights discussion is the desire for owners of content (intellectual property) and users of content to have a reliable mechanism(s) to create, distribute and redistribute intellectual property to any authorized user, anytime, anywhere and on any device and, after distribution, to ensure that content is used as authorized over time.

Although the user requirements and the supplier requirements are not at odds, the current business models and technologies infrastructures available to deliver these needs are incompatible. The struggle to develop new models has created significant confusion and disruption for all parties in the information supply chain—which should perhaps be renamed the information supply grid to reflect the interconnected and nonlinear process publishing has become.

"One of the greatest impediments to realizing the potential of universal access to digital collections, [is] our current system of protecting intellectual property rights. The system works reasonably well—albeit not perfectly—in the traditional analog environment. Transferring the concepts of copyright to the digital arena, however, raises numerous thorny problems."[22]

The notions of what constitutes an author, a publication, a text, for example, do not transfer well from a print world to a digital one. "When theorists talk about the power of the new media to make everyone an author…or to provide everyone with universal access to potential audiences of millions of readers, they invoke a notion of authorship and a model of access that are more appropriate to traditional print media than to electronic communication. What is an author, after all, if the new media no longer support the legal status or institutional privileges that have traditionally defined that role?"[23]

Two models help to visualize the complexity, and most importantly, the tight integration of the many elements of a secure rights management environment.

As the diagram illustrates, the DRM architecture requires a framework that can manage content creation, management and usage. The DRM architecture must ensure security and authentication at each step of the information supply chain.

Digital Rights Management is a nightmare—too confusing.

Corporate Librarian

22. Robert S. Martin, "Reaching Across Library Boundaries," In: *Emerging Visions for Access in the 21st Century Library,* Council on Library and Information Resources and the California Digital Library, Washington DC: CLIR (August 2003): 5.
23. Geoffrey Nunberg, "Farewell to the Information Age," In *The Future of the Book,* ed. Geoffrey Nunberg (Berkeley, CA: University of California Press, 1996): 105.

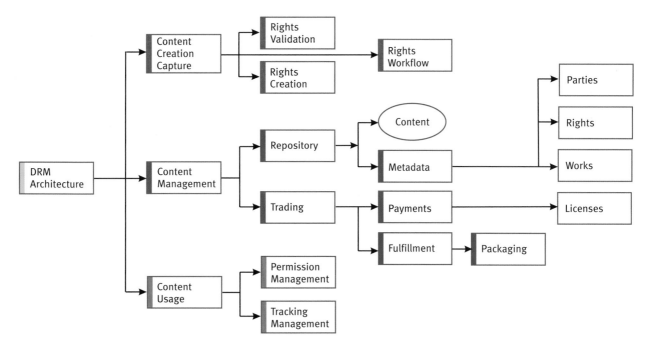

DRM Functional Architecture diagram[24]

Where is scholarly publishing going? Each player says "I want to have control over copyright" but others will want control, too.

Director, Academic Library

A second model, developed by Dr. Mark Stefik, Manager of the Information Sciences and Technologies Laboratory at Palo Alto Research Center (PARC) has been included below to help illustrate the concepts of granting digital rights over the life of an asset.[25]

An effective DRM architecture will not only require secure rights management at the initial content use, but must remain persistent with the content as it is edited or embedded, in the future. Since next-generation applications will reach much deeper into day-to-day activities of consumers, businesses and governments, they will require built-in safeguards far beyond passwords and physical security. That security must "travel" with the asset as it is consumed, reused and repurposed. That security must also support both the user and the owner.

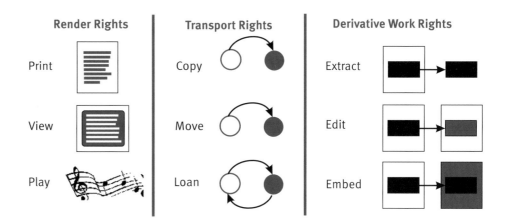

24. Created by Renato Iannella, Chief Scientist at IPR Systems and published in "Digital Rights Management (DRM) Architectures," *D-Lib Magazine* 7, no.6 (June 2001).
25. Published in "DRM Concepts/Standards," *GiantSteps.com,* copyright 2000, GiantSteps Media Technology Strategies, all rights reserved, www.giantstepsmts.com/.

Owner-centric	User-flexible	26
Digital Dog Kennel or Leash (maintain control at all times and all costs)	Digital Dog Chip (digital object identifier links to a database)	
	Digital Dog Tag (metadata and watermarks) but sometimes it also involves Kennel (firewalls, encryption) or a Leash (temporary unlocking key) Free range	
The revenue is made at time of each license	Flexible revenue timing—pay for usage, pay for time, some usage is free	
Financial risk/reward balance is locked at this time	Risk/reward balance can adapt to fit circumstances	
Fixed usages as specified by owner	Flexible, permissible usage travel with objects either directly or via link back to a database (equivalent to a dog's microchip)	
Fixed consumer-oriented licenses	Standard "Nano contracts"	
Owner-centric	User-flexible	

More and more, there is a move from technologies that provide "copyright protection" (owner-centric) to technology frameworks that enable "rights management" (user-flexible). As outlined in the "Digital Dog" chart above, rights management technologies must meld with other trends. Technology analysts are not sure how this melding of technology and user adoption will occur. Many predict that the technical DRM solutions will not mature as separate solutions, but rather will become embedded features within larger enterprise applications and hardware solutions. Intel, Microsoft, Sun and others have plans to implement DRM features in future releases. It is likely that hardware devices, including cell phones and many entertainment appliances, will also embed DRM features and options. The DRM architectures we discussed in this section will be supported by these technical advances but how quickly, and how effectively, remains to be seen. DRM solution adoption will likely be driven more by economics than technologies. It is still early in the "melding process." But as one senior information professional reminds us, "Until a workable approach in addressing intellectual property rights is developed, we cannot realize the potential of digital libraries."[27]

26. Iannella, "Digital Rights Management (DRM) Architectures."
27. Martin, "Reaching Across Library Boundaries."

Which technologies have captured the attention of the information consumer? Four technologies should be on your to-do list for 2004.

Wi-Fi, short for wireless fidelity, is a technology that has captured the heart of the information consumer and is filling tables at coffee shops across the world. Public wireless Internet access via "hotspots" is a customer service technology worth reviewing this year. Many libraries are already experimenting with or implementing Wi-Fi in their institutions. There are security concerns and the relatively short range reach of hotspots and ability to figure out the right financial model are still hurdles to clear. Jupiter Research reports that 6 percent of U.S. consumers have used Wi-Fi services in a public place[1]. Why not make the library the first public place for the next 50 percent?

The high school students interviewed for the scan told us that the technology tool they wanted most was a PDA device that "contained all the information they needed to do their work."[2] Vendors are responding. Several vendors now offer PDAs under $100, making it possible for the information consumer to get a PDA for about the price of two video games. **Personalization, alert technology** and other PDA-friendly information services have brought a world of convenience to the business user. The information consumer is ready for libraries to bring "all the information they need to do their work" to their PDAs.

Smart Cards, the "intelligent" credit card originally launched in the 1980s may finally have its year in 2004. As infrastructure elements come into place and security costs skyrocket, these access authentication mechanisms and data stores are gaining in popularity with both the information consumer and institutions. Universities, banks and governments worldwide are adopting these plastic computers. It is worth exploring how collaborative programs with other local or campus agencies could deliver new and innovative customer services.

1. Matt Villano, "Wi-Fi is Hot but Users Still Warming to It," www.wi-fiplanet.com/news/article.php/3111721 (December 4, 2003).
2. OCLC Focus Groups, Columbus, Ohio (November 12, 2003).

"How close are we to the Semantic Web that [Tim] Berners-Lee describes? Yes, and my American garage door talks to my Belgian toaster, and they agree I am hungry. Great idea. I think it will take a long time to realize, and that we will go through several generations of enabling technologies before we find ones that are suitable to actually get the job done."[28]

Herbert Van de Sompel

Hype or hope?

Our review of the technology landscape identified four major trends. The first, a rush to find ways to bring structure to unstructured data—giving rise to powerful search engines and the emergence of automatic data categorization techniques. Second, we highlighted the move away from highly integrated technology architectures to more distributed, component-based software solutions and the associated rise in Web services. The third major trend identified is the maturing of open-source solutions as legitimate components to an IT department's technical strategy. Finally, we provided a review of some of potential DRM architectures that may help support the growth of digital libraries.

These four trends may be among the more significant developments shaping the technology landscape, but they represent only a fraction of the technological advancements that information professionals must access and evaluate. While it would be impractical to list the hundreds of emerging technologies and standards uncovered during our research, we want to provide an overview of a few more technologies that we feel may have an impact on the future shape of the information landscape.

We feel it is important not only to identify these technology trends, but to present them in frameworks that information professionals could use to separate "the hype from the hope" of these new and emerging technologies and tools. What tools are being adopted today? Which technologies are not yet ready for prime time, but may shape the landscape in the next 5–10 years? Which of today's hot technologies may not survive?

28. Tom Storey, "An Interview with Herbert Van de Sompel: Developing New Protocols to Support and Connect Digital Libraries," *OCLC Newsletter* No.261 (July 2003): 12.

We conclude our review of the technology landscape by taking a broad look at several of the specific technologies shaping the future of knowledge management. To provide that overview, we use an adoption framework called "hype cycles" that was developed by Gartner, Inc., the world's leading technology research and advisory organization.[30] Widely used today to help technology professionals assess the maturity of emerging technologies, the hype cycles can provide an interesting view of many of the technologies impacting areas of interest. Gartner provides over 100 hype cycles to its clients. They have granted OCLC permission to use two of those hype cycles for review in this report: the Hype Cycle for Knowledge Management and the Hype Cycle for Web Services.

The Hype Cycle for Knowledge Management, 2003 identifies 23 technologies or solutions that Gartner feels will influence the future development of knowledge management. To understand a technology or technical solution's placement on the curve is a helpful management device. Gartner has added the element of "human attitude" or "market hype" to the traditional production adoption curve to allow information managers the opportunity to factor in the impact of hype, both positive and negative, on strategic investment decisions. Four of the solutions on the Hype Cycle for Knowledge Management—packaged methodologies, document management, best-practices programs and Web content management—have reached the "plateau of productivity" phase on the curve, indicating that they have been adopted by at least 30 percent of the market and are being deployed today as knowledge management enablers. Gartner plots the remaining 19 of these technologies at various points on the curve and indicates their estimated "time to plateau." Certain technologies, such as personal knowledge networks and corporate blogging, are very early in the cycle according to Gartner. Others have passed through the "peak of inflated expectations" and are perhaps currently no longer making press headlines, sitting in the "trough of disillusionment." Automated text categorization, discussed earlier in this section, is located in the trough. Gartner suggests that these technologies should not necessarily be discounted simply because they have fallen from the headlines as they may provide interesting potential that could be realized in a more quiet phase of the adoption cycle. According to its placement on this chart, Gartner estimates that automated text categorization will reach the plateau of productivity with the next two to five years.

Several of the top trends and technologies identified in this scan—e-learning, taxonomies and collaboration techniques—are plotted on the Knowledge Management Hype Cycle.

In the Hype Cycle for Web Services, 18 technical solutions are plotted to provide a guide to the ever-growing number of Web services solutions that are available today or will be available in the next decade. Web services tailored for specific industries and applications as well as Web services for infrastructure, security, networking and portals, all appear to be on the horizon.

Since 1995, Gartner has used hype cycles to characterize the over-enthusiasm or "hype" and subsequent disappointment that typically happen with the introduction of new technologies. Hype cycles show how and when technologies move beyond the hype to offer practical benefits and become widely accepted. Gartner currently offers over 100 hype cycles to their clients covering a vast array of technologies including: Web services, XML technologies, open-source technologies, advanced analytics, application development, mobile and wireless networking, personal computers and more.[29]

For more information see: www.gartner.com

---

29.   Definitions of the different phases of a Gartner Hype Cycle are included in the Glossary, pp. 113–23.
30.   A. Linden and J. Fenn, "Understanding Gartner's Hype Cycles," *Strategic Analysis Report,* R-20-1971 (Stamford, CT: Gartner, Inc., May 30, 2003): 6.

Hype Cycle for Knowledge Management, 2003[31]

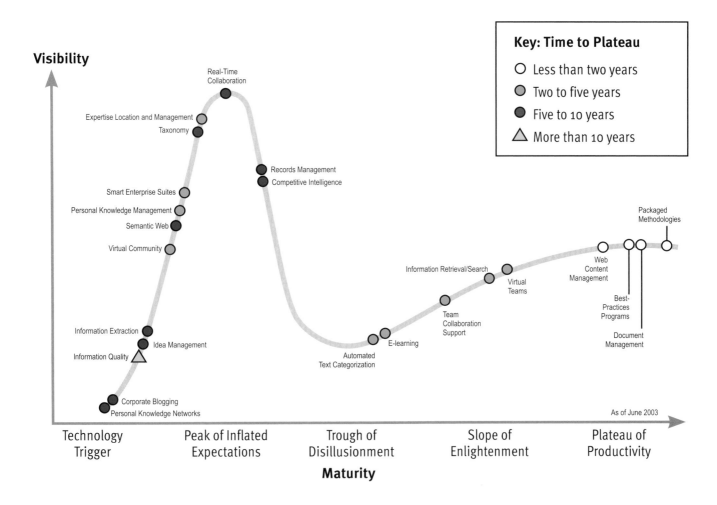

Key: Time to Plateau

○ Less than two years
◐ Two to five years
● Five to 10 years
△ More than 10 years

Visibility

Real-Time Collaboration
Expertise Location and Management
Taxonomy
Records Management
Competitive Intelligence
Smart Enterprise Suites
Personal Knowledge Management
Semantic Web
Virtual Community
Information Retrieval/Search
Virtual Teams
Team Collaboration Support
Web Content Management
Packaged Methodologies
Best-Practices Programs
Document Management
Information Extraction
Idea Management
Information Quality
E-learning
Automated Text Categorization
Corporate Blogging
Personal Knowledge Networks

As of June 2003

Technology Trigger | Peak of Inflated Expectations | Trough of Disillusionment | Slope of Enlightenment | Plateau of Productivity

Maturity

Terminology definitions

Personal Knowledge Networks
Virtual networks centered on individual knowledge workers

Corporate Blogging
The application of "Web log" styles to corporate objectives

Information Quality
A characteristic that makes information suitable to support knowledge work

Idea Management
A process for developing, identifying and using valuable insights

Information Extraction
Culling concepts from unstructured data

Virtual Community
A self-selecting, peer-to-peer group that connects people by interest, skills and practices

Semantic Web
Extends the Web through semantic markup languages that describe entities and their relationships

Personal Knowledge Management
Powerful KM systems on the desktop

Smart Enterprise Suites
The convergence of portals, content management and collaboration functionality into a single product

Taxonomy
A classification of information components and the relationships among them

Expertise Location and Management
A tacit knowledge capture and sharing process

Real-Time Collaboration
Interaction between participants in real time using a meeting or presentation format

Records Management
The management of knowledge content through its complete life cycle

Competitive Intelligence
The analysis of an enterprise's business environment

Automated Text Categorization
Use of statistical models or hand-coded rules to rate a document's relevancy to specific subject categories

E-learning
The use of electronic technologies to deliver cognitive information and training

Team Collaboration Support
Tools that bring together real-time communications and asynchronous collaboration for teams

Information Retrieval/Search
The retrieval of documents based on a metric applied to a user's query

Virtual Teams
A project-oriented group of knowledge workers who do not physically work together

Web Content Management
Controlling Web site content with specific tools

Best-Practices Programs
A process of capturing and sharing process-oriented knowledge

Document Management
A server-based repository that offers library services

Packaged Methodologies
Capturing and using process-oriented knowledge

31. F. Caldwell and others, "Hype Cycle for Knowledge Management, 2003," *Strategic Analysis Report,* R-20-0010 (Stamford, CT: Gartner, Inc., June 6, 2003).

Hype Cycle for Web Services, 2003 [32]

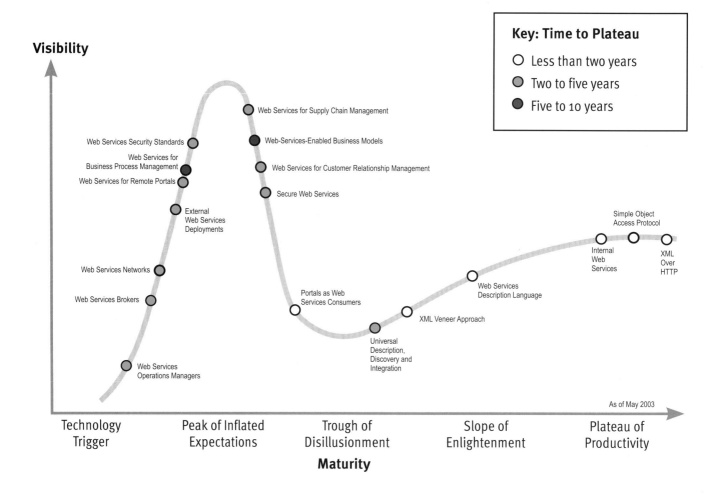

32.   Whit Andrews and others, "Hype Cycle for Web Services, 2003," *Strategic Analysis Report* (Stamford, CT: Gartner, Inc., May 30, 2003).

Terminology definitions

Web Services Operations Managers
Address out-of-band management of Web services

Web Services Brokers
Provide security and deliver intelligence for internal Web services

Web Services Networks
A brokering service that supports digital collaboration between applications

External Web Services Deployments
Web services that provide data interchange and application integration

Web Services for Remote Portals
A common means for portals to obtain and display information

Web Services for Business Process Management
Web services used to circumscribe and initiate business processes

Web Services Security Standards
Standards that establish methods through which Web services can be connected securely

Web Services for Supply Chain Management
The use of Web services technologies to improve connections for buying and selling

Web Services-Enabled Business Models
Approaches for doing business impossible without the benefits of Web services

Web Services for Customer Relationship Management
CRM applications serving as producers or consumers of Web services

Secure Web Services
Implementations of Web services that resist computer attack

Portals as Web Services Consumers
The use of an enterprise portal through which the results of Web services are displayed

Universal Description Discovery and Integration
A type of service to publish, search for and use Web services

XML Veneer Approach
Uses XML to transport data without using Web services

Web Services Description Language
A formal XML vocabulary and grammar that describe, discover and use Web services

Internal Web Services
The use of Web services to accomplish noninvasive integration

Simple Object Access Protocol
Allows one application to invoke a remote procedure call on another application

XML Over HTTP
Uses XML and XML standards, but not Web services standards

Implications

- The emergence of Web services and the movement away from stovepipe, monolithic applications will likely make distributed applications more achievable than older distributed application models, such as OSI or CORBA. *How do libraries take advantage of these new technologies and new architectures to deliver new or additional services?*

- The increased importance of open-source software and changes in the way organizations create, distribute, acquire and exploit software are providing new opportunities for industry. *What new opportunities exist for libraries to work together to build more open-source solutions?*

- Building flexibility and responsiveness into processes, products and organizational structure will be required to take advantage of many of the emerging technologies—going "permanently beta" may be the trend. *What organization or staffing changes will be required for libraries to operate in these new, less formal structures?*

- The change in the nature of ownership of intellectual property has driven many technology companies as well as content companies to invest in digital rights management solutions. *What DRM solutions will be required to meet the unique needs of libraries and which technologies will simply become part of the "general information exchange infrastructure"?*

- There will be increased autonomy and independence for regions and countries as the dependency on expensive, monolithic technical systems declines. *What challenges, and what opportunities, does this create for increased collaboration of libraries around the world?*

The Research & Learning Landscape

Patterns of change in the research and learning landscape cover not only the institutions engaged in research and learning, but also encompass research and learning practices of individuals. Learning is a process that can take place in designated primary, secondary and tertiary institutions of learning, and it is also a self-directed, personal process, as well as a workplace activity. All these kinds of research and learning activities impact libraries and allied organizations. The aim of this section is to identify the most important trends of the changing research and learning landscape as they may impact these organizations.

Major trends

- **Reduced funding**
- **Proliferation of e-learning**
- **Lifelong learning in the community**
- **The changing pattern of research and learning in higher education**
- **Institutional repositories, scholarly communication and open access**
- **New flows of scholarly materials**

Reduced funding

Consistent with trends we examined in The Economic Landscape, the areas of K–12 and higher education are experiencing reduced funding as governments struggle to constrain expenditures without increasing taxation.

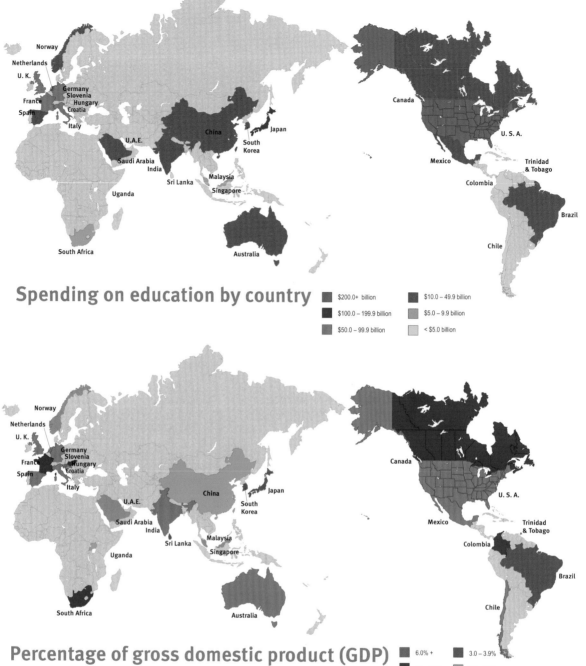

Spending on education by country

■ $200.0+ billion	■ $10.0 – 49.9 billion
■ $100.0 – 199.9 billion	▨ $5.0 – 9.9 billion
■ $50.0 – 99.9 billion	▨ < $5.0 billion

Percentage of gross domestic product (GDP) spent on education

■ 6.0% +	■ 3.0 – 3.9%
■ 5.0 – 5.9%	▨ 2.0 – 2.9%
■ 4.0 – 4.9%	▨ < 2.0%

Country education spending

Country	Education Spending (Billions)	% GDP on Education	Country	Education Spending (Billions)	% GDP on Education	Country	Education Spending (Billions)	% GDP on Education
United States	$ 500	4.8%	India	$ 21	4.1%	Hungary	$ 3	5.0%
Japan	$ 139	3.5%	Netherlands	$ 20	4.8%	Singapore	$ 3	3.7%
Germany	$ 89	4.5%	Australia	$ 19	4.7%	Chile	$ 3	4.2%
France	$ 82	5.8%	South Korea	$ 18	3.8%	U.A.E	$ 1	1.9%
United Kingdom	$ 70	4.5%	Saudi Arabia	$ 18	9.5%	Slovenia	$ 1	4.9%
Italy	$ 54	4.6%	Brazil	$ 17	3.8%	Croatia	$ 1	4.2%
Canada	$ 39	5.4%	Norway	$ 13	6.8%	Sri Lanka	$ 0.5	3.1%
Spain	$ 29	4.5%	South Africa	$ 6	5.7%	Trinidad & Tobago	$ 0.4	4.0%
Mexico	$ 28	4.4%	Malaysia	$ 6	6.2%	Uganda	$ 0.1	2.3%
China	$ 27	2.2%	Colombia	$ 4	5.1%			

Source: UNESCO Institute for Statistics (May 2003).

Library directors are increasingly focused on fund-raising.

Director, Academic Library

In the United States, the situation is unlikely to change any time soon. According to the National Center for Public Policy and Higher Education, all but a handful of states will find it impossible to maintain current levels of public services within their existing tax structures.[1]

These projections suggest that the fiscal prospects for higher education are not rosy. At the same time, there is a strong interest in increasing access for qualified students as the "branding" of the value of higher education is firmly embedded in the social fabric. Calls for accountability and measurability mentioned in the Economic Landscape are loud and clear in the research and learning landscape.

"We can no longer put billions of dollars into the system without expecting colleges to become more affordable. We can never give enough aid if colleges just keep raising their prices. The federal government will continue to do its fair share to help bridge the financial divide between what families can afford to pay for college and what they are expected to pay. We will support those institutions that are trying to make college less expensive. But because the federal government provides 70 percent of all financial aid, it is time for Congress to demand accountability. We must seize this opportunity and ask colleges to do their part in increasing access to higher education."[2]

Viewed solely through a funding lens, the future of education looks pretty dismal. And indeed, if the structure and organization of educational institutions remain as they are today, the future is likely not rosy.

"If we are worried about the declining state of education and decreasing state and federal budgets, disruptive innovation could be a powerful new framework for the debate over how best to improve primary and secondary schools. If the debate is framed around preserving the status quo, then disruptive innovations are of little use. However, if the debate is framed around how to provide the best quality instruction at the lowest possible price to the greatest number of people, officials should find a way to encourage the creation of disruptive business models. Successful disruptive business models will fling open the doors of quality education to previously underserved and nonconsuming populations. Moreover, social and economic welfare will increase as more people learn at all educational levels."[3]

Proliferation of e-learning

E-learning might be one of the disruptive innovations in education. It now has a presence in most large corporations and in an ever-increasing number of college and university courses. In this section we look at general trends in e-learning as a delivery mechanism.

Once synonymous with distance learning, e-learning has quickly evolved to include not only courses that are taught primarily online and over a distance, but also those that include traditional, "building-based" courses that have been enhanced with electronic elements. These "hybrid" courses are offered by 80 percent of U.S. institutions, according to a report from the EDUCAUSE

1. Dennis Jones, "State Shortfalls Projected Through the Decade," *Policy Alert* (February 2003).
2. Howard P. McKeon, "Controlling the Price of College," *The Chronicle of Higher Education* (July 11, 2003): B20.
    (McKeon is the Chairman of the House Subcommittee on 21st Century Competitiveness and has introduced the College Affordability in Higher Education Act.)
3. Clayton M. Christensen, Sally Aaron and William Clark, "Disruption in Education," In *The Internet and the University Forum 2001* (Boulder, CO: EDUCAUSE, 2002): 41.

Center for Applied Research.[4] However, the number of such courses offered is still only a small percentage of all courses offered.

Not surprisingly, there has been a parallel growth in the number of institutions using course management systems to manage hybrid courses' electronic elements. They have moved swiftly from scattered implementations that support a few online classes to enterprise-wide services that support and extend the entire curriculum and related institutional services. Course management systems such as WebCT and Blackboard allow for the creation of a virtual classroom where faculty and students can interact and post curriculum-related material.

E-learning in the university[5]

Universities have had a difficult time making distance education cost-effective and pedagogically effective because they usually tried to deliver traditional courses via a nontraditional medium. As Christensen points out in "Disruption in Education"[6] the failure of this sort of online learning was that, essentially, it delivered a course to consumers who experienced it as a lesser and unsatisfactory version of a campus-based course. Newer models of nonclassroom-based education do not try to duplicate the classroom environment but instead embrace technology as a way to reach students.

University of Phoenix, The Netherlands—Graduation MBA 2003

More than 170,000 students are currently enrolled at the 134 campuses and learning centers of the University of Phoenix, making it the largest private institution in the United States.

www.universityofphoenix.com

The University of Phoenix was one of the first institutions to use the Internet to deliver course material at a time when other providers were shipping physical books. Founded in 1976, it was one of the first accredited universities to provide college degrees via the Internet to students who would not be able to attend classes on a physical campus, for reasons of time, geography and preference.

Another more recent entrant into the "disruptive online learning" space is Universitas 21 (U21), a consortium of international universities offering postgraduate online courses. The first degree program is an MBA. "It is estimated that the e-learning market in the Asia Pacific region will reach US$400 million by 2005. That's two years from now. Depending on living standards, fees vary across countries. So an Indian pays US$11,000, while a Singaporean US$13,000 [...] Dr. Mukesh Aghi, CEO of Universitas 21 Global, said: 'There are roughly 35 million students who are unable to get that education and that number will grow to 100 million in 10 to 15 years.' The institution said it would not mimic a traditional brick and mortar university and so there won't be any video-conferencing. While doing assignments, students can access articles, journals and periodicals in the online library. But they won't be able to gain access to the libraries of participating universities."[7] Students will, however, be able to access content provided by Thomson Learning, through Thomson's proprietary learning management system.

4. ECAR Respondent Summary: *Evolving Campus Support Models for E-Learning Courses* (March 2003).
5. For a thorough discussion of e-learning in the academic setting at it pertains to libraries, see OCLC E-learning Task Force (Neil MacLean and Heidi Sander, primary editors), *Libraries and the Enhancement of E-Learning,* (Dublin, OH: OCLC, 2003), www5.oclc.org/downloads/community/elearning.pdf.
6. Christensen, et al., "Disruption in Education."
7. Ca-Mie De Souza, "Online university group in S'pore invests $50m to sell courses to Asian students," *ChannelNewsAsia.com* (September 7, 2003).

Centrally stored materials that can be repurposed might be sensible.

Academic Librarian

Creating, managing and delivering content in an e-learning environment requires the conscious and planned collaboration of several sectors of a university's community. Faculty, IT staff, administration staff and librarians all have roles and responsibilities in content management; however, these sectors have generally worked relatively autonomously from one another. Cooperation and collaboration become crucial.

It is not only the organizational elements of a university that must work together to deliver content successfully and effectively to students. Learning materials themselves must, in a sense, collaborate. In the past, if a history professor used the Shakespeare play *Titus Andronicus* to illustrate a particular point about warfare, she did not take the classroom material—the learning object—created by her colleague the English professor on the same play and repurpose it for her needs. In a pedagogical world supported by an enterprise-wide course management system, this becomes possible, and perhaps, desirable. These learning objects need to be managed just as the books in the library do.

Learning objects

Learning objects are the basic electronic building blocks for e-learning. They are sharable, fine-grained materials that can be recombined and reused in different course offerings. In this sense, learning objects are "multicultural." In an ideal world, learning objects can be used over and over, and can be combined with other learning objects to make new ones.

Learning object repositories are emerging at the campus level and in wider settings. For example, CAREO (Campus Alberta Repository of Educational Objects—www.careo.org/) is a project supported by the provincial government education department, Alberta Learning, and CANARIE (Canada's advanced Internet development organization) that has as its primary goal the creation of a searchable, Web-based collection of multidisciplinary teaching materials for educators across the province and beyond.

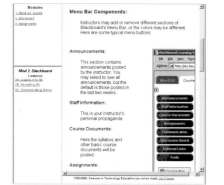

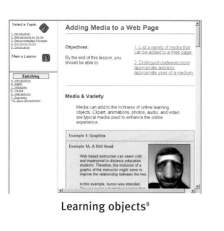

Learning objects[8]

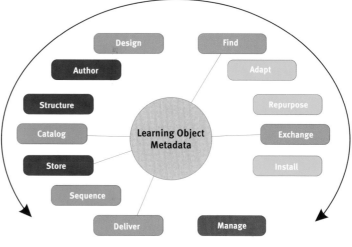

Learning object life cycle diagram[9]

8. Learning objects courtesy of Dr. Jim Flowers, Department of Industry & Technology, Ball State University.
9. Learning object life cycle picture courtesy of Dan Rehak, Carnegie Mellon University.

E-learning in the workplace

E-learning is also the term used to describe corporate or work-based e-learning. In 2001, estimated worldwide revenues for 2004 for corporate e-learning were just over US$23 billion dollars, up from less than $2 billion at year-end in 1999.[10] Companies purchase e-learning for workers for many of the same reasons that individuals take university courses online: travel time is reduced, infrastructure costs are low, delivery is platform independent and learning anywhere and anytime is enabled.

E-learning is big business. In the September 1, 2003 issue of *Fortune,* the 100 Fastest Growing Companies are profiled. Number 4 and number 6 are e-learning companies: Career Education (revenue: $849.3 million) and Corinthian Colleges ($472.9 million). Both offer postsecondary courses to a combined total of over 100,000 students on more than 150 campuses.

Overall, there's a lot of internal resistance [at the press] to any e-learning initiatives due to status quo thinking.

University Press Editor

Lifelong learning in the community

"We often hear it said that libraries (and librarians) select, organize, retrieve and transmit information or knowledge. That is true. But those are the activities, not the mission, of the library. Certainly we perform those activities, but the important question is: To what purpose? We do not do those things by and of themselves. We do them in order to address an important and continuing need of the society we seek to serve. In short, we do them to support learning. [...] We must create a learning society."[11]

A learning society, lifelong learning, learning for life, the knowledge-based economy: the emergence of learning as an important political agenda has challenged libraries, museums and related organizations to show that they can make a difference, that they add value, that they are central to educational and civic missions. This is a common international theme, played out in different social and political contexts. Interestingly, this theme emerges at the same time as a more general questioning about the value of public goods and the open availability of resources.

Learning is an issue that resonates throughout social and political discussion.

A knowledge economy

A knowledge economy is a general label for an economy in which technology and the knowledge on which it is based are central motors of economic growth. This means that a growing number of workers manipulate symbols rather than machines. And it means that human or intellectual capital—the knowledge that comes from education, training, on-the-job experience and workplace-based e-learning—is central to sustaining personal and organizational advantage.

10. IDC, *Worldwide Corporate eLearning Market Forecast and Analysis,* 1999–2004 (2001). As quoted by Cerint Technology Group, www.cerint.com/company/The_Worldwide_Corporate_eLearning_Market-IDC.pdf and Margaret Driscoll, IBM Mindspan Solution.
11. Robert S. Martin, "Reaching Across Library Boundaries," *In Emerging Visions for Access in the 21st Century Library,* (August 2003): 11.

Library and communities

This economic shift has some implications:

- The ability to learn and to adapt to change is a central life skill. Learning is valued as a crucial coping skill in an environment of change and flexibility.

- There is growing fragmentation between those who are connected and those who are unconnected, where "connection" literally and metaphorically stands for social inclusion, in terms of access to life skills, opportunity and the instruments of learning.

The library can be a resource to other community agencies in information management.

Director, Public Library

- The global network is enabling interest communities to collaborate in real time on a planetary scale. This has been visible with large corporations and financial markets where information flows without recognizing borders. Research communities and other groups benefit from the ability to work together. At the same time, there is a resurgence of interest in regional and local identities as the world is recast as a network of regions and cities, as a sense of community and belonging becomes more important against this globalizing background. There is a growing desire to reclaim the local, to make local history and heritage resources more visible. New forms of community and identity are being forged around affinities of religion, politics, gender and lifestyle, and find support in network frameworks. Blogs and discussion groups are examples.

- The role of public services in the digital environment is under scrutiny. We can see countervailing trends. On one hand there is a general focus on access, on digitizing heritage collections, on making available the results of government-funded research, on providing learning and community resources. An especially interesting issue here is the emergence of home-schooling, and the corresponding lobby to have educational materials available on the network to support progressively advancing learning and teaching needs, particularly in math and sciences. On the other hand, there is a progressive commoditization of knowledge, a desire to restrict access to materials, through licensing and fees.

Libraries in the community

Libraries of all types seek to build the relationships and provide the services that create value to their communities, and which corroborate their role as trusted hubs of community and learning. This involves supporting the variety of learning experiences actively, in working with others to create the visible fabric of community, and in continuing as unobtrusive agents of social cohesion and personal fulfillment.

Here are some roles libraries play:

- Equalizing access in a fragmented society. Libraries have always supported the development of reading, writing and communication skills as well as the development of learning and information skills.

- Supporting the learning experience. Libraries, museums and related organizations are more consciously providing instruments for self-directed learners and curriculum support materials, and are teaching people to be learners. They recognize their complementarity to the formal learning process.

- Globalization and regionalization. The library is a gateway to global resources as a "gone digital" organization, but at the same time it acquires strong regional and local purpose—whether as part of a university with business, learning and cultural links, as a state or regional library that assumes the role of disclosing the business, historical and cultural identity of its area, or as community venue for reading sessions for dogs, belly dancing and meetings of the local DAR.

- The library, historical society and archive have a role in describing the explicit relationships and objects that are evidence and witness of a community and its sense of itself, or rather of the multiple communities that share any library. Local history records, sport, art, culture, social activities: these can be noted, described and shared. Individually such services provide value; made available as a network resource and brought into the same context of use as other such resources, that value is much enhanced.

Libraries are an important part of the civic fabric, woven into people's working and imaginative lives and into the public identity of communities, cities and nations. They are social assembly places, physical knowledge exchanges, whose use and civic presence acknowledge their social significance and the public value accorded to them. In many countries throughout the world, they form a widely dispersed physical network of hospitable places, open to all. Every library is different, but to enter any one is to come home, to experience a "third place" whose mission is defined by service, where people can work unobserved and can develop as they wish. This trusted community role places libraries in a unique position to support the lifelong learner.

> *Libraries need to collaborate to create "whole cloth" collections irrespective of location or holding library.*
> **Public Librarian**

> *The staff has an emerging role in assisting the public in using electronic resources. The principle is that, in the public library, you learn, you are not taught. The librarian's role is to facilitate self-learning, not to act as a teacher.*
> **Public Librarian**

The changing pattern of research and learning in higher education

As part of a university or college, the academic library is not an end in itself. It supports research, learning and scholarship, and it has always had to adapt as research and learning behaviors change. However, in the current network environment, this change is uneven and uncertain and poses great challenges for libraries.

"I assume that university libraries will adapt to change in education and research institutions as they are transformed through the digital revolution."[12] However, as we have seen in our discussion of trends in the social and technology landscapes, learning behaviors of young people— both students and faculty—have changed a great deal, and the institutions supporting their research and learning for the most part have not changed to accommodate the newer members of this community.

"The current generation of scientists is much more familiar with PubMed and Google than the contents of their library shelves."[13]

We can't develop and enforce policies for collecting institutional content beyond our own domain.

Government Librarian

Infrastructure changes

There is a growing investment in learning management systems to mediate and manage the learning experience. Learning materials are being produced in various digital forms and need to be managed. Faculty are creating, analyzing and using digital resources in many ways. Scientific research is being transformed and there is huge investment in large-scale computing infrastructure to support new modes of working. Change may be slower in the humanities and social sciences, but is significant.

In general, the system of scholarly communication is being transformed in unpredictable ways.

Universities are taking a stronger interest in managing their own digital assets, and, in making them more widely available, the library has the opportunity to become involved at various stages, looking at taking on broader institutional asset management responsibilities.

Research is increasingly being carried out in groups, and across historically defined disciplines and also across institutions.

The library is becoming more engaged with the research and learning behaviors of its users, and is supporting them at more stages in their work. Libraries are working in new partnerships with faculty and students and developing new models of academic support.

Libraries, academic computing, administrative computing, educational technology and sometimes the campus bookstore, media services and university press are increasingly being gathered organizationally under one senior university administrator. Where such alignment is not organizationally enacted, libraries and other services are recognizing their overlapping interests and the need for partnership.

12. Robin Stanton, "Towards Supported 'Communities of Interest' in Digital Environments," In: *Emerging Visions for Access in the 21st Century Library* (2003): 33.
13. Susan R. Owens, "Revolution or Evolution?" *EMBO reports* 4, no.8 (2003): 741-3.

"I see a great opportunity for the next five years for a more rigorous and pragmatic partnership between librarians, IT professionals and scholars. While that may sound obvious, it really has not been done."[14]

And finally, there is an emerging emphasis on integration among systems that support learning, research and administration, and a corresponding interest in campus architectures, repository and portal frameworks, and common services such as authentication and authorization.

This technological movement is changing the way faculty and students access, create and use information resources and is creating new support challenges. Among these are questions of how best to support the life cycle management of learning materials; how to develop greater systems integration among learning management, library and administrative systems; and how to diffuse information skills throughout learning activities.

Computing and its supporting infrastructure have evolved steadily and rapidly for 50 years, but the impact on scholarly research methodologies has become particularly evident as these changes have surfaced in ubiquitous personal computing capabilities and high bandwidth connectivity.

Grid computing (http://www.gridcomputing.com) is a strong manifestation of these trends. This community promotes the development and advancement of technologies that provide seamless and scalable access to wide-area distributed resources. Computational grids enable the selection and sharing of geographically distributed computational resources. The idea has become popular in a variety of academic research environments, including computer science, molecular modeling and drug design, biophysics and high-energy physics.

The key to having the library a player in the institutional repository is to have recognized the trend early, and to "work the room" early.

Director, Academic Library

Impact on the sciences

The impact in the sciences has been greater than in the humanities and social sciences. The ambitious recommendations of the NSF Cyberinfrastructure Advisory Panel[15] give an indication of directions science and technology research might go. The report points to the major opportunities for research that emerge from the ubiquitous availability of broadband computing, from the generation of massive amounts of data and from visualization and simulation. It highlights the strong trends in current research towards federation of distributed resources (data, content collections and computing facilities) and distributed, multidisciplinary expertise.

Currently these trends are exemplified in projects and programs involving aerospace research, earth sciences and ecological studies, physics and energy research, biomedical informatics and advanced computing initiatives. The close connection of research and education is particularly critical in this context. Success will depend on providing high-quality educational opportunities necessary to the support of any advanced work. But in addition, the expanded scope and intrinsically distributed, multidisciplinary character of these trends will present particularly novel challenges that must be met with innovative educational technology and management and

I think it would be beneficial for librarians and publishers to work more closely together to identify consumer needs and content delivery systems.

University Press Editor

14. Chuck Henry, "Redefining the Role of the Library," [interview] *Ubiquity* 4, no.25: n.p.
15. Daniel E. Atkins, et. al., *Revolutionizing Science and Engineering Through Cyberinfrastructure,* Report of the National Science Foundation Blue Ribbon Advisory Panel on Cyberinfrastructure (January 2003).

funding. The report also identifies fundamental risks that imperil such progress, including the loss of poorly-curated data, lack of standardization of data formats and poor coherence among IT research, the IT industry and domain science.

The panel proposes the establishment of the Advanced Cyberinfrastructure Program to be funded at an annual level of US$1 billion to address these opportunities.

Home page of the International Poster Collection, created by the Colorado State University Libraries and the Department of Art.[16]

Impact on the humanities

Research in the humanities is changing as well. Though its scope and character are on a smaller scale than the massive, distributed science research projects, humanities and social science research increasingly rely on the availability of information on the scholars' desktops.

The proliferation, especially in the humanities, of new varieties of scholarly artifacts—software, interactive components and multimedia objects—presents novel impediments to discovery, access and preservation of such materials. Wendy Lougee points to the importance of new collaborations between cultural stewards and scholars as essential to the survival of the objects of their stewardship.[17]

The shift of librarianship from a role of service provider to collaborator will be particularly important if the many new varieties of scholarly output have any hope of being cataloged and therefore disclosed to potential users, and preserved in ways that will sustain their value to future scholars.

Libraries and archives contain many of the primary materials upon which research in the humanities is based. However, access to these materials is often inhibited by limited or absent cataloging or finding aids. This makes the collections available to those who already know about them, or who come across them serendipitously. This in turn limits scholarship or teaching based on those materials. It is clear that there is still a major descriptive challenge ahead for libraries, which will involve looking at descriptive practices and looking at greater investment in collection-level description.

Access to materials

The policies and techniques for capturing, sharing and preserving scholarly assets are as yet undeveloped, but Abby Smith[18] classifies approaches to these problems in two categories:

- Enterprise-based model—essentially, institutions assume responsibility for preserving and managing these artifacts, perhaps in the institutional repository.

- Community-based model—third-party stewardship that emerges from a community or discipline. ARTstor is an example of this model.

16. Colorado State University Libraries, International Poster Collection (2001), http://manta.colostate.edu/posters/.
17. Wendy P. Lougee, *Diffuse Libraries: Emergent Roles for the Research Library in the Digital Age* (Washington, D.C.: Council on Library and Information Resources, 2002).
18. Abby Smith, *New Model Scholarship: How Will It Survive?* (Washington, D.C.: Council on Library and Information Resources, 2003).

The underlying challenges and opportunities share common threads, including the obvious themes of rapid technological change and how such changes influence the needs and expectations of researchers and users. Perhaps the deeper themes, however, involve the social and institutional changes necessary to effect the transition from traditional resources, tools and services for support of scholarship to the digital, distributed, seamless environments that will be necessary in the future.

Institutional repositories, scholarly communication and open access

The changes discussed in this section will have a profound impact on the creation, communication and reuse of research and learning outputs. This in turn will have a profound impact on how libraries are organized and the services they provide.

Institutional repositories[19]

There is an growing interest in the more coordinated management and disclosure of digital assets of institutions—learning objects, data sets, e-prints, theses, dissertations and so on. This movement is in early stages and there are no settled patterns or standards. Recently, the term "institutional repository" has emerged as a general summary label for a range of supporting services the library might offer in this environment, working with faculty to provide curatorial attention to a dispersed, complex range of research and learning outputs. DSpace is an initiative of MIT and Hewlett-Packard, providing open-source software for institutional repository development, and importantly, a policy framework for thinking about the development and management of such repositories. Many academic libraries are planning institutional repository initiatives, and many of them are using DSpace.

The most significant challenge facing academic libraries undertaking these institutional repository projects is not technical, however. The major challenge is cultural. Too few initiatives include all the stakeholders—faculty, library staff, IT staff and instructional designers—and there is no common view of what an institutional repository is, what it contains and what its governance structure should be. Faculty have rarely involved librarians in developing teaching materials, digital or otherwise, and have not routinely made these available within the library infrastructure. Librarians have not routinely created metadata for such material.

Scholarly communication

Clifford Lynch directs our attention to the rapid rise in prominence of institutional repository technology as a primary signal of the changing needs of supporting scholarly communication. He applauds these developments, but also points to some of the inherent dangers that attend the evolution of new technology models. High among the risks he sees is the danger of broken promises—the possible discrepancy between the institutional commitments and organizational limitations.[20]

Open access and the institutional repository are huge trends but likely in ways we don't even know. Libraries are reinventing the wheel by trying to take on the roles of publishers. It's like a morality play: reclaim good and leave evil behind.

Director, National Licensing Project

---

19. The OCLC E-learning Task Force White Paper discusses the topic of content management and institutional repositories in more detail. www5.oclc.org/downloads/community/elearning.pdf.
20. Clifford A. Lynch, "Institutional Repositories: Essential Infrastructure for Scholarship in the Digital Age," *ARL Bimonthly Report* 226 (February 2003): 1–7.

A major issue here is that the outputs of digital scholarship are often in complex and nonstandard forms. We do not have routine ways of managing new media. The academic community will need to develop a better understanding of ways in which scholarship and learning activities are created, used, reused and preserved in the digital environment, and of the relationships and infrastructure necessary to sustain these activities.

Open access

The institutional repository discussion is sometimes connected with an "open access" discussion. Open access is concerned with better and broader access to research and learning outputs. More specifically, it is interested in reducing the economic barriers to such access. Examples are:

Libraries need to be proactive about e-learning and not wait to be approached as a partner.

Academic Librarian

- SPARC, the ARL-initiated effort to facilitate competition in scientific communication through the creation of high-quality alternatives to commercial titles and SPARC Europe, recently launched to provide a European operational arm for SPARC activities.

- The establishment of institutional- and discipline-based archives that allow public access to content and employ the Open Archives Metadata Harvesting Protocol.

- PLoS, the Public Library of Science, a nonprofit organization of scientists and physicians committed to making medical and scientific research publicly searchable and accessible.

The open access community is a broad-based movement with significant library support. See in particular the work of ARL in supporting SPARC, and the formation of the International Scholarly Communications Alliance (ISCA) by major library organizations worldwide that are dedicated to the pursuit of Open Access. The development of systems of e-print archives is supported by national initiatives in several countries.

Finally, we note a related set of discussions about access to the outputs of publicly funded research, and a strong desire to see those freely available to those whose tax dollars have supported the research in the first place. In the U.S. this discussion has been focused by the legislation introduced in Congress in June 2003 by Rep. Martin Olav Sabo (MN) to make papers written to report results of work funded by federal agencies free of copyright. Needless to say, this has generated a good deal of both pro and con discussion.

It is worth keeping in mind that the revolution in scholarly publishing and communication is now almost 15 years old. So far, the system of measuring and rewarding academic staff at universities has changed very little. This is a very complex ecosystem and adjusting one part of it does not necessarily yield the desired results. As one former academic pointed out in an interview with OCLC staff: scholarly publishing in journals has an archival function to it overlooked by many debates about open access to scholarly research. Researchers in specific fields do not rely on published articles to keep up. "Keeping up" is done through preprints, e-mail and personal Web sites.

New flows of scholarly materials

It is clear that a new ecology and a new economy for scholarly information are being formed. At this early stage the players are working through issues, roles and responsibilities, models, territorial disputes and change. Because there is a lot at stake, it is difficult to know how things will turn out. We have moved from a landscape with well-understood contours to one that is still "under construction." The following figure (adapted from Lyons[21] with permission) aims to show how the new environment might look. Changing research and learning behaviors results in a flow of research and learning outputs that, in turn, form the inputs for new research and learning activities. In the past, such flows tended to be concentrated through formal, linear publishing mechanisms; we are now seeing the emergence of a variety of repository frameworks, metadata aggregation services and richer content interconnection and repurposing that are changing how we think about data and its uses. Elements in the flow include:

- **Repositories.** These may be institutional, personal[22] or community-based. They may be disciplinary or general. They may be specialized by format or general. (Try using Google to search "personal repository."[23])

Too many digital resources have been initiated by some entrepreneurial activity that is not sustained by real need or a community of interest.

Director, Funding Agency

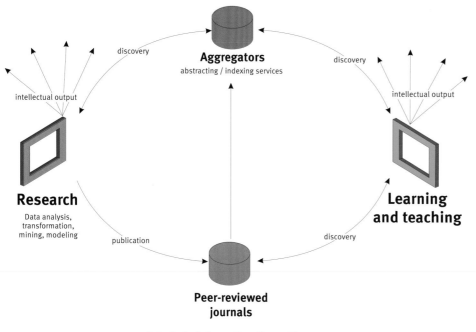

Scholarly information flow—Then

21. Liz Lyon, "eBank UK: Building the links between research data, scholarly communication and learning," *Ariadne* 36 (2003), www.ariadne.ac.uk/issue36/lyon/.
22. MyLifeBits is a Microsoft project for storing all of one's digital media, including documents, images, sounds and video.
23. www.archivists.org/publications/donating-familyrecs.asp.

- **Aggregator services.** These may be commercial services or provided through community or central funding of some sort. ResearchIndex (formerly CiteSeer) is an interesting example of a popular aggregator for particular disciplinary communities.

- **The library.** Clearly, the library potentially intersects with this cycle at many points: as a manager of institutional repositories, as a licensor of external services, as a facilitator for deposit or self-archiving, as a local persistent repository provider. The role of the library as aggregator has yet to be worked out. But, the library has the opportunity to take a leadership role in developing policies and programs that contribute to a coherent, institution-wide knowledge management system.

Libraries are ideally placed to continue to build relationships and to provide the services that create value to their communities, and which corroborate their role as trusted hubs of community and learning.

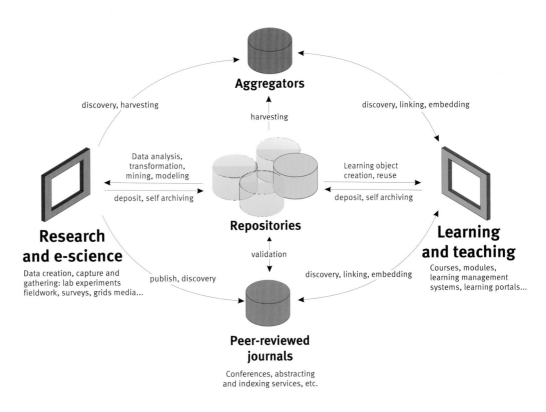

Scholarly information flow—Now

Implications

- There needs to be a reexamination and refocusing of the roles of public services in support of lifelong learning and scholarship. *What are the points of contact between libraries and museums, public service broadcasting and education?*

- There is a widening gap between library services and systems and those in the e-learning and scholarly communication landscapes. *How do libraries of all types align themselves with the e-learning communities?*

- New learning and research needs may not be met by legacy services. *What services are required to support an informed citizenry, to create learning and creative opportunities?*

- New models of learning, research and scholarly communication will drive changes in the institutions that support this activity. *What changes should be made to the organizational structure of such institutions?*

- Changes in learning, research and scholarly communication will require that librarians become literate in information, collection and service architectures, and contribute to the design of such architectures. *How should library education change and adapt to accommodate these changes?*

- Lack of data format standardization, loss of poorly digitized and curated data, and lack of a common IT infrastructure imperil progress in integrating the assets of the cultural heritage and scholarly environments. *Given that there is likely to be little new money for asset management of digital material, how will libraries and allied organizations preserve, curate and provide access to digital collections?*

The Library Landscape

The Library[1] Landscape section was the most challenging of the six landscape sections to compile—not surprisingly perhaps, because it is the landscape with which OCLC and its membership are most familiar and it both deserves and will get particular scrutiny with regard to trends. None of us is unaware of the trends outlined below and many, many interesting, thoughtful and scholarly articles have been published on these and other relevant topics.

As you read this section reflect not so much on these trends, which may tell you nothing new (think of them as reminders), but on the

Sustainability is only possible through collaboration.

gaps or synergies you notice that relate to the other landscapes. An early reader of one of the landscapes remarked "But there's nothing new here. I know all this stuff already." And the response was a gentle, "But isn't that the problem?" If we do see the patterns of our own landscape, what has been done to address the challenges?

And so, familiarity with this landscape may mean it is actually more difficult to recognize the overarching trends—the major patterns threading their way through the fabric—because we are so familiar with each of the trends highlighted, as well as all those not mentioned. It is, perhaps, only the contrast between or the relationships among these trends to other trends identified in the environmental scan that will lead to pattern recognition.

---

1. "Library" is used here as shorthand for libraries, archives, museums and historical societies.

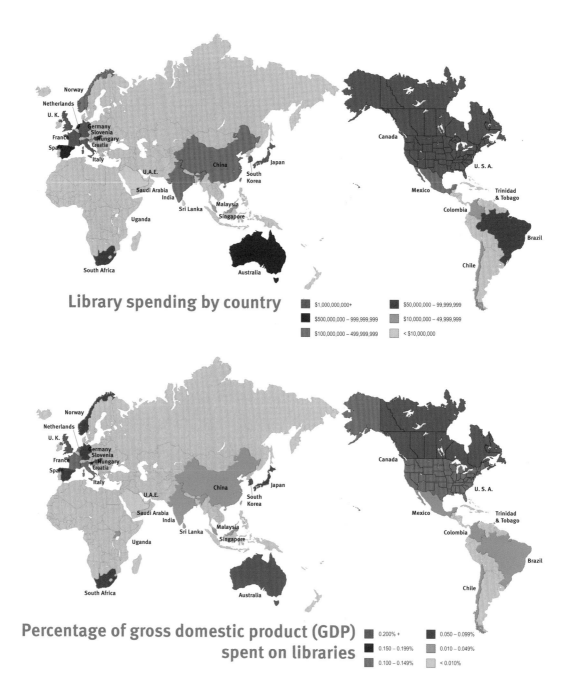

Library spending by country

$1,000,000,000+	$50,000,000 – 99,999,999
$500,000,000 – 999,999,999	$10,000,000 – 49,999,999
$100,000,000 – 499,999,999	< $10,000,000

Percentage of gross domestic product (GDP) spent on libraries

0.200% +	0.050 – 0.099%
0.150 – 0.199%	0.010 – 0.049%
0.100 – 0.149%	< 0.010%

Country library spending

Country	Library Spending (Millions)	% GDP on Libraries	Country	Library Spending (Millions)	%GDP on Libraries	Country	Library Spending (Millions)	% GDP on Libraries
United States	$ 11,951	0.11%	Spain	$ 531	0.08%	Malaysia	$ 28	0.03%
Japan	$ 3,247	0.08%	China	$ 218	0.02%	Colombia	$ 16	0.02%
United Kingdom	$ 3,221	0.21%	Norway	$ 179	0.09%	Chile	$ 13	0.02%
Italy	$ 1,599	0.14%	Mexico	$ 104	0.02%	Croatia	$ 8	0.04%
France	$ 1,591	0.11%	India	$ 103	0.02%	Saudi Arabia	$ 7	0.00%
South Korea	$ 1,507	0.32%	Brazil	$ 90	0.02%	Sri Lanka	$ 3	0.02%
Canada	$ 1,447	0.20%	Singapore	$ 70	0.08%	Trinidad & Tobago	$ 3	0.03%
Germany	$ 1,353	0.07%	South Africa	$ 68	0.06%	U.A.E.	$ 3	0.00%
Australia	$ 834	0.20%	Hungary	$ 64	0.10%	Uganda	$ 1	0.01%
Netherlands	$ 536	0.13%	Slovenia	$ 35	0.17%			

Source: Various including LibEcon, UNESCO, *World Encyclopedia of Library and Information Services* and estimates for certain countries.

It is worth repeating from the quote at the beginning of this landscape scan: "Our accumulation of and intense focus on our knowledge controls what we believe. And, what we believe controls what we are able to see. What haven't you noticed lately?"[2]

This section is structured slightly differently from the other sections. It is divided into two subsections: The Social Landscape and The Technology Landscape. The subsection titles deliberately use the titles from earlier sections that are, in a sense, the larger frameworks of the library environments. The social and technology landscapes within the library landscape cannot exist independently of the larger ones and are—or should be—informed by trends in them.

The Social Landscape focuses on the people, content and issues that make up the Library Landscape.

The Technology Landscape focuses on the hardware, software and infrastructures that make up the Library Landscape.

The Social Landscape

Primary research informs this subsection of the scan. OCLC staff interviewed almost 100 people in a wide variety of institutions, organizations and positions to gather information and opinions for this section.[3]

The framework of the interviews was set using the Collections Grid developed by Lorcan Dempsey and Eric Childress of OCLC Research, and a series of questions that was sent to each interviewee prior to the actual conversations.[4] Some interviews were conducted in person, but most were done by telephone. Not all interviews followed the structure suggested by the questions, and some interviewees did not want to answer the OCLC questions but wanted to talk about other issues. As a result, unexpectedly, the transcripts of the conversations contained material relevant to all

2. Federman, "Enterprise Awareness."
3. Please see "People Consulted" on pp. 127–31.
4. Please see the "Collections Grid" and the questions on pp. 125–26.

sections in this report. All of the interviews yielded a huge amount of interesting and insightful comments on the real, day-to-day issues facing information professionals working in libraries, archives, historical societies, museums, and allied organizations and companies. It is worth noting that the people interviewed are almost all Baby Boomers (born from 1946–1964) and as such, their points-of-view are of people probably in the last third of their professional careers.

It is here in this social landscape that the information gathered during the interview process is best represented, although it has been used throughout the report as well. The narrative is informed by the thoughtful insights of the information professionals interviewed, and the bullet points represent paraphrased remarks from the interviewees. There were divergent views expressed about what needs to be done, who is responsible for activities and projects, and no consensus evident. There was however one central unifying theme to almost all of the interviews: this is the twilight zone. For the Baby Boomer generation of information professionals at least, clarity of purpose has blurred.

Major trends

- **Staffing**
- **New roles**
- **Accommodating users**
- **Traditional versus nontraditional content**
- **Preservation and persistence**
- **Funding and accountability**
- **Collaboration**

Staffing

Much has been written and spoken about the demographics of librarianship in the past few years. Some of it has had the tone of a Chicken Little story: the sky is falling. As the Baby Boomer librarians and paraprofessionals move through their careers like a bulge in a well-fed snake[5] they worry about the apparent vacuum left by their imminent retirements. Certainly, in not so many years, a huge amount of collective experience and knowledge will be gone from cataloging departments and reference desks. At the other end of the age scale, there are not enough young librarians entering the profession to replace the retirees. Professions evolve and need to evolve and the changing demographics of this landscape will provide serious challenges to institutions. At the same time, there are and will be opportunities to restructure and change. And as we saw in the Economic Landscape, libraries worldwide continue to spend a great deal of their financial resources on staffing. Library staffing shortages could allow libraries to reorganize more

5. The Editor acknowledges this image comes from Samuel Rothstein, one of her professors at UBC.

easily and hire specific and new skill sets. As they always have, young staff lend a great deal of energy and enthusiasm to their workplaces.

Here are some key points about **staffing** made by people OCLC interviewed:

- Early adoption of innovations means a need for positions filled by highly trained staff who often cost more than "regular" staff.

- A lot of staff will retire soon but the upside to this is being able to hire staff more comfortable with **e-material and virtual services**.

- Too much staff time and effort is spent on trying to **organize free Web content**. Why do we need to do this?

- It's hard to get older staff to **consider acquiring "unpublished" material**.

- Libraries should reallocate positions to newer kinds of jobs: **digital scholarship**, open-source projects, etc.

- More and more library directors are **not librarians or academic staff**— does this matter?

- Young librarians may be more willing to design systems that **meet users where they are** rather than the way it is now—we want the users to come to us.

- Librarians aren't rewarded for **risk-taking**—the organization favors the status quo.

- Succession planning? None.

- **We're well aware of trends and issues** but many staff are not truly willing to change the ways they do things.

There's so much
going on...
I want to
do it all!

Serving you
better, seeing
you less.

Anatomy of a Gen X librarian: "Energized and excited"

Profile:

Female, age 28
Librarian, Communications Studies

Education:

B.A. History—University of Idaho,
MLIS University of Washington

Learning style:

Learns by doing, not by "seat" learning

Favorite pastimes:

Antiquing

Reading

The Generation X librarians have been part of the workforce for a few years and are an energetic and ambitious group. At 28, this Gen X librarian describes herself as "energized and excited." In her interview with OCLC, she said "There's so much going on, so many unconnected and different initiatives—and I want to do all of them!" In her opinion, funding reductions to libraries won't stop projects. It'll just be a bit harder to get them funded and more grants will have to be applied for. "But," she said, "We weren't trained how to do this at library school and maybe we should have been. Seeking alternative sources of funding is a necessary part of my job, and it takes a lot of time. And the amounts awarded are often so small I sometimes think it would be faster and easier just to pay for something myself." This altruistic and do-it-yourself approach is typical of people younger than 30. "Libraries should pool their money and share the wealth."

She believes that libraries of all types have to collaborate to market their joint services and make sure their collections complement, not overlap. "When I do bibliographic instruction, I tell my students to go to the public library, for example, because it has great sources that we don't have here on campus. I think the differences between kinds of libraries are blurring and that's good. Seamlessness is what we're aiming for—we don't want users to have to pick what libraries or librarians to go to when they have questions. That's why virtual reference has so much potential. Why should a person have to select one of the 18 libraries on campus before she can ask her question?"

Baby Boomer librarians have had to work hard to stand out in their crowded workplaces and like to put their own mark on things. Our Xer librarian said:

> ### *"Collectively, we feel we need to do everything ourselves—we need to get over this.*

We've spread ourselves too thin. Now, we're not the only ones who know about metadata, or searching, or creating Web pathfinders. If I can find a great pathfinder on another library's Web site, I'll simply link to it. I certainly don't need to redo their good work."

When she was asked what she thought about Boomer librarians, she said, "Boomers have gone through drastic changes, and some are just exhausted and cynical, but some are still very excited about their work. I've learned so much from the Boomer librarians that I work with. They're great colleagues and mentors. Maybe the generation gap is more about energy than age."

And what does a young librarian see as the profession's major challenges?

> ### *"Working collaboratively with people to make things happen.*

Here on campus, we don't work together enough. The faculty, the IT staff and librarians have a fantastic pool of knowledge and expertise, and if we worked together on the big stuff—digital scholarship is an example—we would get things done faster and better. And we wouldn't have to figure everything out by ourselves. We're really great at talking about what needs to be done, but then we all go back to work. There's too much day-to-day work to work on the high-level challenges. It would be great if we found a better way to communicate and then actually solve the problems that we've spent countless hours discussing."

What about that day-to-day work, Gen X librarian? "Regular work, such as filing microfilm, keeps me grounded. I love contact with students. I am really reassured and energized by what I see when I teach. Seeing students 'get it' is so rewarding."

So what does a Gen X librarian think of the Web? "I like the Web and appreciate the amount of information that's available there. But, students are not well served by the open Web. They'll look through the first five results and take the best of those five. I work with faculty to create assignments that require sources that students won't find using Google." Well, in this, our Gen X librarian seems to be much like librarians of any age. And perhaps this is why we don't need to worry about the future of the profession. Gen X and Millennial librarians may be more comfortable with change and technological gadgets than their Traditionalist and Boomer compatriots but at bottom, they seem to be very much like we all were at their ages. The Boomer OCLC interviewer and Gen X interviewee had a laugh over a common experience separated by almost 20 years: both had embarrassing moments in front of a class of students when, in an effort to be hip, they used search terms that immediately labeled them as completely out-of-touch with those 19-year-olds. The terms "yuppies" and "Ferris Bueller" got equally blank stares from across the generational divide. Our Gen Xer librarian has a solution: "I subscribe to *Entertainment Weekly* to keep in touch with students."

New roles

"[T]he new [Salt Lake City Main] library is a secular city center where groups of all ethnicities, religions, politics and purposes feel they have a place and a stake. The library hosts classes in English as a second language, meditation and Braille, as well as discussion groups about the latest nonfiction. Organizations from Weight Watchers to the Royal Court of the Golden Spike Empire to No More Homeless Pets have held meetings in the building, as well as Amnesty International, Single Moms, the Hispanic Dance Alliance and the Utah Socialists. On Saturdays, a group meets to read to their dogs."[6]

Among the many new roles libraries are assuming is the role of Library as community center. Not just warehouses of content, they are social assembly places, participating in their larger communities by building information commons, hosting poetry contests, digitizing city council minutes and positioning themselves as the knowledge management experts within their peer groups. In some respects, the goal of being relevant to one's community is no different from the earlier goals of any broad-minded and sensible administrator. But, in an era when public support of institutions like the library and the local park is under scrutiny, a reliance on citizens funding an institution they may use infrequently is likely not good planning. Funding bodies demand to see tangible, measurable returns on their investments and busy libraries suggest money well spent. It makes a great deal of sense for libraries to look for new, broader service opportunities within their communities.

Here are some key points about **new roles** made by people OCLC interviewed:

- The library should serve as a **community/civic center**.

- There is an opportunity for the public library to be the **aggregator of community information and partner with other local organizations** to gather grey literature.

- There is demand for 24/7 access to the physical library as well as the virtual one—I call this **"retail expectations."**

- **Access is a form of sustainability**. Content that can be accessed is valued and is more likely to be sustained by the community.

- The hard work of collection development is not with published material; it is with **new formats and delivery mechanisms**.

- Archives are seeing a big drop in "turnstile traffic" due to **self-service** via the Web.

- Mass-market materials are increasingly **avoiding traditional distribution channels** such as the library.

- **Collections are increasingly generic**—even among research libraries— as standard aggregated content is bought. There is a focus on **merchandising the reading experience**—book superstores introduced this and did an outstanding job. Libraries were built to accommodate materials management, not users.

6. Mary Brown Malouf, *The Salt Lake Tribune* (August 25, 2003), www.sltrib.com/2003/Aug/08252003/utah/86808.asp.

- The library can be—and should be—**a resource to other community agencies** for information management.

- Libraries need to work with a **broader group of agencies**.

- Libraries need to be **proactive about e-learning** and not wait to be approached as a partner.

Accommodating users

"Internet-savvy students told us that the online world offers many advantages over the alternatives—school-issued textbooks and their school and community libraries. They said the Internet is much easier and more convenient to access. It is as close as the nearest Internet connection—which is often in their homes—and does not require a ride in a car or bus. Students said school and community libraries have limited selections of multimedia, while online sites routinely offer downloadable graphic images, photographs, animations, video and sound. However, a unanimous "no" echoed throughout the OCLC focus groups when we asked if they are able to complete their entire projects on the Internet. 'You still need a lot of resources,' said one student."[7]

"Senior citizens, at the other end of the spectrum, told us their primary reasons for going online include doing e-mail, reading newspapers and searching for information on prescriptions, finance and investments, hobbies, recipes, movies and garage sales. They told us the reasons they use the library include book sales, taking grandchildren to reading programs and reading newspapers. 'Computers are kind of a shortcut to information. They really are. But, I still think the library and the printed word…you have to have that, too,' said one senior."[7]

While there are some outstanding examples of libraries making efforts to take services and content to users, it is still the case that most library users must go virtually or physically to the library. Library content and services are rarely pushed to the user although more and more libraries are using RSS feeds and content packaged for handheld devices as a way to get into users' spaces.

Here are some key points about **accommodating users** made by people OCLC interviewed:

- We need to stop looking at things from a library point of view and **focus on the user's point of view**.

- Users don't care if content is a Web page, a blog, a book or a serial.

- A common interface to content is not a big deal anymore.

- **Personalization and categorization** are really important for the end user as a way of filtering through large sets.

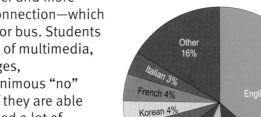

Top ten spoken languages [8]

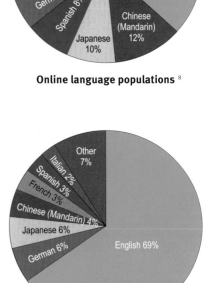

Online language populations [8]

Languages of Web content [8]

7. High School Students: The Internet and Information Use, OCLC Focus Group (November 2003).
    Senior Citizens: The Internet and Information Use, OCLC Focus Group (November 2003).
8. For sources consulted, see "Sources" on p. 147.

- Undergraduates are using a lot more primary material.

- Librarians **underestimate users' knowledge** of searching the Web—how did we learn to read newspapers without help? Aren't they collections of unrelated material too?

- There is a high level of **satisfaction with self-service** applications in libraries.

- Librarians **cannot change user behavior** and so need to meet the user.

- Vendors are always looking to see how people's needs are not being met and stepping into that hole—libraries don't do this. They try and make the people fit the library.

- Libraries are behind the curve—services have not been built to support user interests.

- Use drives selection—**convenience is more important** than it was. Convenience of service has increased as an expectation from the public, as they expect hours of service to match retail hours of service.

- We confuse building-based services with services in general. Why should a user care if content comes from the law library or the medical library?

*Big bookstores are excellent at
merchandising the reading experience.
Most libraries were designed
for materials management.*
Director, Public Library

Traditional versus nontraditional content

"It was the best of times, it was the worst of times."[9] Perhaps none of the trends covered here fits this notion better than trends in content. All of the pressures inherent in the landscapes covered in the scan converge here. Social, economic, technological and learning issues make content management for libraries and allied organizations enormously challenging. The older pre-Internet world of content coexists with the new world. Print material must still be bought, circulated, reshelved, repaired, preserved and discarded. This material will persist, much of it will not be digitized and people will continue to use it. But, because libraries do not exist independently of their cultures, all artifacts of those cultures must be curated, preserved and made accessible. So, the challenges faced by the stewards of content will not diminish, and issues of description, use and preservation will be radically different than the issues related to the print content currently under stewardship.

Clifford Lynch makes this point unambiguously; "Rather than considering how to redesign or recreate or enhance libraries as digital libraries, we might usefully focus our attention on the human and social purposes and needs that libraries and allied cultural memory institutions have been intended to address. [...] [W]e must be careful not to overly emphasize the parts of this knowledge ecosystem that are familiar, that we are comfortable with intellectually, socially and economically, to the exclusion of the new, the unfamiliar, the disturbing, the confusing."[10]

Here are some key points about **content** made by people OCLC interviewed:

- Being **collection-centric is old-fashioned**; content is no longer king— context is.

- **Context** means adding intellectual value to content.

- Maybe it would be cheaper to **buy monographs as POD** (print-on-demand) rather than buying in anticipation of need.

- Most libraries' status is about what they own. How can we change this? It is the library equivalent of the tenure system.

- We need a way to **bring together all content** on a topic, not just what's in the catalog.

- The library has no curatorial role for published material—**it's up to third parties to archive**.

- Bibliographic information is a **corporate asset** and should be treated like other assets.

- Librarians are way too focused on published material: they should **leave that to the Amazons** and concentrate on the hard stuff.

- Special collections need to be **liberated and desegregated**.

The library as a book warehouse is passé.
Director, Academic Library

We're trying to create an edge in electronic publishing and take advantage of opportunities, but the challenge is how to do that when revenue is flat.
University Press Editor

9. Charles Dickens, *A Tale of Two Cities.*
10. Clifford Lynch, "Reflections Towards the Development of a 'Post-DL' Research Agenda," paper presented at the National Science Foundation invitational workshop, Post-Digital Libraries Research Futures (Chatham, MA: June 15-17, 2003), www.sis.pitt.edu/~dlwkshop/paper_lynch.pdf.

Today's community information is tomorrow's cultural heritage.

Print on demand could be huge.

- Access to published content is closing down as **licensing restrictions increase**.

- The idea of the **balanced—but unread—collection** is disappearing.

- The Web means public libraries can **focus more on specific, local communities**—we can be more specialized. There is no need for all branch libraries in a system to have a common core collection.

- **Print-on-demand** could be huge.

- Publishers and librarians need to **work more closely together** to identify consumer needs and content delivery systems.

- There is a lot of interest in **deconstructing the publishing unit**.

- We need to provide **what the market wants** but we haven't established what that is.

- Librarians avoid talking about relationships among content and certainly have not done anything about this.

- Creation of copy cataloging is not a sustainable model—there is **less and less need for human-generated cataloging** and less ability to pay for it.

- The goal should be **access to print** material and **stewardship of institutionally published material**.

- Institutional repositories are important but we're not doing anything. **We're waiting** to see what others do.

- **There is no consensus** as to what institutional repositories are.

- Who has or will have the large-scale utilities for **data migration** of the content of institutional repositories?

- My library today is more like Harvard than it was 20 years ago because of the **common aggregated material.**

- There must be **more linkages among content types**—people should be able to find all relevant material regardless of what content quadrant it belongs in.

- Institutional content may never be "collected" but the library should have a **curatorial role**.

- **Simple indexing and ranking** are good enough for open Web resources— get over the cataloging issue!

- **Collection-level records** have to be the way to go for large, related collections.

- Much institutional repository work is bypassing the library.

- We definitely have **no consensus** or idea what to do about material on the open Web.

- The jury's out on the sustainability of e-learning but publishers are looking at **repurposing content** for course packs.

- Publishers are slow to see the need for **languages other than English**.

- We need to get medical and engineering content to underdeveloped nations—this could be a **big growth area**.

Preservation and persistence

Issues set out in this section are, in effect, a subset of the issues outlined above in content management. How will content be preserved, archived and represented to users now and in the future? Issues related to persistence and preservation of content are perhaps thornier than the broader issues related to content selection, description and management because even in the older world of exclusively print collections much talk resulted in little activity. As one interviewee said so succinctly: "There is no more substance behind 'digital preservation' than there was behind 'print preservation.' All talk about how important it is and we don't do either. Besides, there's no money for preservation of any type." As is evident from the points made by interviewees, there is perhaps even less agreement about the nature of the challenges inherent in archiving and preservation than there is in other areas.

Here are some key points about **preservation and persistence** made by people OCLC interviewed:

- Digital preservation has to be a **national issue**—it will never work on an institution-by-institution basis.

- Preservation of institutional content is the responsibility now of the parent institution—it's a **huge burden.**

- We haven't a clue how to approach digitization. Thematically? Chronologically? **Cataloging does not help** with such decisions.

- Digitization is for **dissemination, not preservation**.

- Digitization is basically a **cottage industry**, institutionally driven and based on no standards.

- **We haven't preserved print** so why the big concern about digital preservation?

- There is a **chaos of creation** out there—everybody's creating digital content—we desperately need some system of archival value assessment.

- It is **not cost-effective** for each library to digitize—it must be a national effort.

- **Why preserve** something if it was not durable in the first place?

- Preservation is **more about social relationships** than formats and technical issues.

- There are **no standards** and no national strategy for preserving cultural heritage.

- Access licenses have effectively taken the discussion of preservation out of the realm of the possible—we don't own the content and we can't archive it.

- **Access is a form of sustainability**—content that can be accessed is valued and is more likely to be sustained by the community.

- **We're all saving the same stuff**—we need a national last copy and preservation program.

- Paper content is being moved off-site to make room for things like cafés and information commons, but **what stays and what goes**? We do not have good tools for these decisions.

- The technology infrastructure isn't a big deal anymore—**technology happens**. But Digital Rights Management (DRM) and identity management are big deals.

- There is an **overwhelming tension** between the DRM community and the open access community and it's getting worse.

- DRM is **hugely complex** to manage and coordinate—we need standardization!

Funding and accountability

"Libraries are becoming less viewed as a community resource than they used to be, in part because chain bookstores are kicking their butts in that area, providing a place to read, chat, have a coffee and even attend events. Maybe it's chicken and egg, because **if libraries were better utilized they'd probably get more funding**. I don't know if that's the issue. So libraries need to improve their current public image, from boring, dusty 'whispering-only' collections of old books, to cool places to check out the latest books from your favourite author. Basically that's what the large bookstores are doing. Knowing that the library has copies of *recent* books is important, and borrowing the coffee shop idea from the chain stores is not a bad idea either!"[11]

Funding to libraries, museums, historical societies and other institutions reliant on the public purse may continue to decline in the short term. Libraries have been responding to reductions in funding by closing for some specified time, reducing programs, reducing staff hours and forgoing materials purchases. There is another trend: competition among sister institutions for funding. In one Ohio county, a private library strapped for funds and in danger of having to drastically reduce staffing and hours of service, appealed to the County Budget Commission for funding. They were successful in getting a share of the state library subsidy, but at the expense of two public libraries in the county. The amount awarded to the private library was deducted from the amounts allocated to the public libraries. As a result, the public libraries will have to determine what to cuts to make up for the unanticipated shortfall in funding.

11. Posted on Slashdot (http://slashdot.org) by "silk" (Sunday, August 24, 2003).

This example pits a private institution against public ones, but extrapolating from this budgetary battle suggests the possibility of county systems competing with city systems, with liberal arts college libraries vying with large academic libraries, with school libraries forced to merge with public libraries. There may be benefits to such joint-use libraries.

Here are some key points about **funding and accountability** made by people OCLC interviewed:

- Technology issues are not difficult, **funding is**.

- Librarians have **unrealistic expectations about pricing** of content—they do not understand the economics of publishing.

- Print revenue can't be artificially protected by trying to make e-content mimic p-content—one user, one book doesn't make sense for e-books.

- E-content has done nothing to help **cost control of materials.**

- We need changing measurements of **library performance** resulting from the growth of electronic services.

- **Donors are very keen** to have their collections digitized—libraries should use them for funding.

- Library directors are increasingly focusing on **fund-raising**.

- Special collections are increasingly important and could be a **source of revenue**.

- Libraries and archives may have to **sell valuable collections** to fund other collections and projects.

- Governments are questioning the **value/cost/benefit** of higher education versus vocational education.

Digitization is not necessarily a preservation method.

Do collaborative collection development.

- We need **flexible e-commerce models** for content—would you subscribe to Lands' End?

- Better automation for **assessing ROI is crucial** for identifying what was bought and how it was used.

- Economies of copy cataloging have diminished as much content now shares little characteristics with traditional, published material.

- Accountability is really important—better your Board gets **information on material usage** than hear about it in the press.

- **Budget reductions** at institutions put centrally-funded collections at risk: national money builds collections, local money supports buildings and physical access so even if we keep national money, reductions in local funding jeopardize collections.

- The public won't support endeavors they can't see.

Collaboration

"[I]f the last few decades of library and information developments have taught us anything, then it's surely that the really significant advances, and the most meaningful and lasting solutions, are cooperative ones. And more than that: they are tending to become global ones. MARC, AACR2 and even the Internet itself, are obvious examples of this, and there are many others; and the rise of consortia of every kind is testimony to the growing recognition of the value—the necessity even—of interinstitutional cooperation, at both local and international levels. [...] I hope we can all agree that, even where we are in competition, we also have a mutual self-interest in helping to build systems and processes and models and service-delivery solutions that are based on cooperatively-agreed solutions and standards."[12]

"It's possible for people of varying levels of technical skills to build useful tools and applications in a spirit of informal collaboration and fun; that software development doesn't have to involve a lot of top-down planning, RFPs and whatnot."[13]

Here are some key points about **collaboration** made by people OCLC interviewed:

- Smaller institutions should **work together** on institutional repositories because we're too small to have our own.

- **Joint use of libraries** is something smaller institutions need to look at— combined academic libraries, combined school/public libraries, combined public/academic libraries.

- **Libraries need to collaborate** to create "whole cloth" collections irrespective of location or holding library.

12. Reg Carr, *The Future of Libraries and Collections: Keynote address to the Fiesole Collection Development Retreat*, Oxford (20 July 2000), www.bodley.ox.ac.uk/librarian/fiesole/fiesole.htm.
13. John Durno, speaking about Hackfest 2003 held during the Access 2003 conference in Vancouver, BC, quoted in Roy Tennant, "Where Librarians Go to Hack," *Library Journal* (e-version) (November 15, 2003), www.libraryjournal.com/article/CA332564.

- Libraries should **explore the affiliations** of their parent institutions for funding and collaboration opportunities—alumni are more likely to support activities related to special purposes.

- Centrally-stored (i.e., at the state or national level) materials that can be repurposed might be sensible.

- **Shared preservation is crucial**—can we get by with ten copies instead of 500?

- We need **way more collaboration** among museums, libraries and historical societies to present coherent collections.

- Historical societies could be **much more visible** by partnering with public libraries to digitize local historical materials.

- Collaboration comes with a cost—institutions have to **share priorities**, and coordination takes staff time.

- We need to share off-site storage and **do collaborative collection development**—there's too much for any one institution to do.

- A collaboration between the city and the public library only **increases the value of the library.**

- Overlapping public libraries—county and city—need to **collaborate to decide how to maximize strengths** and not duplicate work and collections.

- Local history collections often are not all that unique. The material is elsewhere—local historical society, university library, state library—and so **inventories must be done** before expensive digitization projects are done.

- OCLC's role is to provide interinstitutional collaboration— **be a collaborative not a cooperative.**

Sustainability is only possible through collaboration.

The Technology Landscape

"New applications of technology will enable libraries to shift from their traditional emphasis on the packages of data to furnishing information for decisions and action.

Hence, the new technology will provide librarians with the opportunity of developing new concepts of librarianship, having as their main emphasis the provision of information to individuals when and where they need it.

Finally, it must be recognized that this new librarianship will evolve step-by-step and in cadence with the cultural evolution of our society."[14]

Fred Kilgour, 1981

Major trends

The library applications environment is poised in a very interesting way. Long dominated by the Integrated Library System, we are finally seeing a necessary move to a more plural systems environment. This is accompanied by two complementary trends. First, really distributed systems look as if they will emerge at last. And second, many library protocols and standards are being modernized in a "Webby" idiom, making them less library-specific. Accordingly, this section is written around four dominant themes:

- **An increasingly interconnected environment**
- **Network services and architecture**
- **New standards**
- **Universal access to information**

An increasingly interconnected environment

The library systems environment is becoming more densely interconnected. This is a result of several pressures:

- The need for more systems support for the range of library activities in a digital environment.

- The evolution of consortial and other shared arrangements.

- The need to interconnect with nonlibrary systems such as learning management systems or campus portals.

- The use of common services such as authentication across applications.

14. Frederick G. Kilgour, "The Next Fifty Years in Libraries," *Reed* 59, no. 10 (May 1981): 11–4.

Systems Support

The first area of pressure is the diversity and number of systems that information organizations may have. Consider the range of systems investments libraries now potentially make to support their operations:

- **Library management system.** Long the core of library automation, the sector is served by a range of well-known companies that specialize in library management solutions.

- **Digital object management system.** As libraries digitize their collections or look to managing other digital objects they need to put in place systems support. Digital asset management systems are now a commodity. Some are generic; some are specialized to the library or cultural heritage communities.

- **Portal or metasearch system.** There are two broad classes of portal applications that have been deployed in libraries: cross-searching systems, using Z39.50 and other approaches, and personalization systems like MyLibrary.

- **Resolver/linker.** This is a relatively new application, but one that has quickly been taken on board by many libraries. A resolver or open linking system allows a library to link a citation or OpenURL to copies of the cited items. This is especially important for the library, which wishes to guide its users to the most appropriate copy of an item, based on cost or policy concerns.

- **ILL/resource sharing system.** Several systems support the management of interlibrary lending transactions.

Most libraries have a library management system. Many will have more than one of the above systems. Some larger libraries will have them all.

An interesting manifestation of this trend is the diversification of product offerings from the major library management system vendors. Although they may be bundled differently, the larger library system vendors now offer digital object management systems, portal systems and resolver systems, in addition to library management systems. Of course, a variety of other providers also make these systems available and in some cases—digital object management, for example—open-source systems may have some impact.

Growth of formalized sharing

The second pressure is the growing trend towards group resource-sharing arrangements, at various levels. Depending on circumstances, these may be consortial in nature, or may flow from state, regional or national structures. This has led to several systems solutions.

One is a distributed approach where library systems remain autonomous, but employ portal and resource-sharing technologies to provide a "virtual" union resource. This is the approach taken by consortia that implement Fretwell Downing's VDX for resource sharing for example. This depends on complex distributed interactions, using protocols such as Z39.50 and the ISO interlibrary loan protocol.

A second approach is a totally centralized approach. This is not very common, but is implemented by the Norwegian academic system Bibsys for example. Here all the Norwegian academic libraries share the same centralized library system.

A third approach is a hybrid one, a mix of centralized and distributed approaches. This is what we find in OhioLink for example, where libraries have their own local library systems but there is a centralized union catalog and interlibrary "circulation" or ILL system. Another hybrid approach is exemplified in OCLC's group catalog service, where, again, each library retains its own system, but looks to a central resource on OCLC for union catalog and ILL request services. In the hybrid case, the central system needs to communicate with local systems to determine holdings and availability data. In the OhioLink case, all the libraries share the same system, which facilitates this interaction at the cost of uniformity; the group catalog approach is more flexible in terms of local system, but at the cost of complexity of interaction. It requires some protocol support.

Interconnecting and interoperability

The third pressure is relatively new, but will become more important over time. This is the need to interact with other systems' environments. Take two topical examples. The first is the learning—or course—management systems. In academic environments, the library is looking for ways to ensure that its services are visible within the learning environment where students increasingly do much of their work. The leading learning management systems—Blackboard and WebCT especially—are in discussion with library management system vendors about facilitating these links.[15] A second example is the campus portal. It is estimated that two-fifths of campuses in the U.S. will have campus portals by the end of 2003.[16] Increasingly, the library will need to think about how its services are surfaced in those environments.[17]

Finally, library applications increasingly need to interact with "common services"—services that are delivered enterprise-wide. The one of most immediate importance is authentication and authorization, as library users want single sign-on facilities to library resources. Several techniques are in use here, but Shibboleth is emerging as an approach of great interest. This is a common service because it is one that needs to be used by many applications, and one, which, increasingly, it does not make sense to provide on an application-by-application basis.

What we have here then, is a systems environment becoming more and more complex. And these complex systems need to talk to each other in various ways. So, for example, one wants to move content between repositories. A portal application needs to search across a range of resources. A central catalog may need to query a local circulation system for availability data. This in turn raises—much more starkly than in the past—the need for interoperability and a move to thinking about systems as communicating network services.

15. See the University of Edinburgh library's implementation of WebCT: srv1.mvm.ed.ac.uk/devilweb/.
16. "The Campus Computing Project: An Interview with Kenneth C. Green," *Commentary* (November/December 2002), http://ts.mivu.org/default.asp?show=article&id=1055.
17. See the University of Delaware's *WebCT Resources:* www2.lib.udel.edu/usered/WebCT.htm.

Network services and architecture

As the environment becomes more complex, we are seeing a movement away from application "stovepipes" towards a decomposition of applications, so that they can be recombined to meet emerging needs more flexibly. Think of this as repurposing for architectures. An architectural perspective becomes interesting as a way of visualizing the system components and the relationships between them. A simple architectural perspective is presented here as a way of framing some discussion about interoperability.

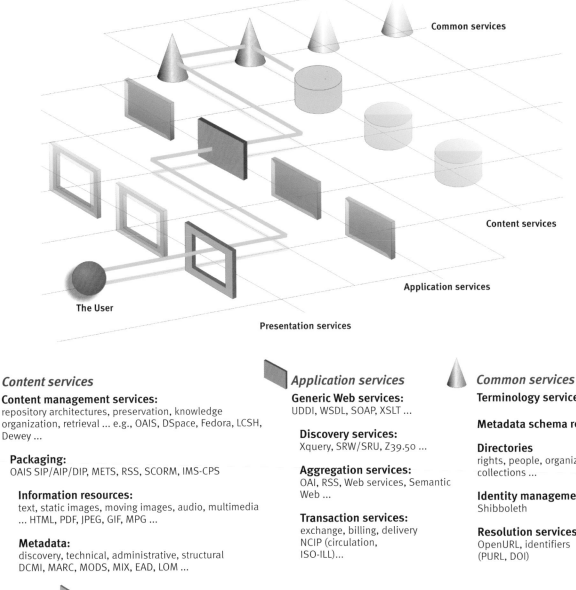

Application architecture

Common services

Content services

Application services

The User

Presentation services

Content services

Content management services:
repository architectures, preservation, knowledge organization, retrieval ... e.g., OAIS, DSpace, Fedora, LCSH, Dewey ...

Packaging:
OAIS SIP/AIP/DIP, METS, RSS, SCORM, IMS-CPS

Information resources:
text, static images, moving images, audio, multimedia ... HTML, PDF, JPEG, GIF, MPG ...

Metadata:
discovery, technical, administrative, structural DCMI, MARC, MODS, MIX, EAD, LOM ...

Application services

Generic Web services:
UDDI, WSDL, SOAP, XSLT ...

Discovery services:
Xquery, SRW/SRU, Z39.50 ...

Aggregation services:
OAI, RSS, Web services, Semantic Web ...

Transaction services:
exchange, billing, delivery NCIP (circulation, ISO-ILL)...

Common services

Terminology services

Metadata schema registries

Directories
rights, people, organizations, collections ...

Identity management:
Shibboleth

Resolution services:
OpenURL, identifiers (PURL, DOI)

Presentation

Rendering:
browser, database interfaces, media players ...

Content views:
personalization, visualization ...

End-user support:
searching, ordering and delivery, technical support ...

This perspective is based on the JISC Information Environment, which looks at how a set of national services might be developed collaboratively, in the United Kingdom, but which has become more widely influential.[18] Effectively, it describes an environment onto which a portal provides a view. Some other architectural perspectives are available. At a high level these architectural initiatives are quite similar, they discuss similar services and seek to facilitate similar types of design and discussion.

What this architectural perspective shows are the following types of services:

- **Presentation services:** these are responsible for accepting user input and rendering system outputs. Typically, services are presented to a Web browser, but other environments (cell phone, PDA, collaborative environments, and so on) are possible. As discussed above, library services may be made available at their own interface, within a library portal, but also increasingly in other environments such as learning management systems, virtual exhibitions or campus portals. The presentation layer may be a "portlet," a channel in some other environment.

- **Application:** these are services responsible for managing transactions between components. In business terms, these are the "business logic." We have already discussed metasearch and resource-sharing applications. Another emerging application is aggregation, where metadata or content is "harvested" into a repository. A question broker is an application, which drives virtual reference services.

- **Content services:** these are repositories of data and metadata. Libraries have always managed large metadata repositories. In the last few years, more libraries are now also managing growing repositories of content. This poses a range of technical and service challenges, as well as preservation challenges.

- **Common services:** these are services that are potentially shared by several applications. They include things like directory or registry services, authentication and so on. A union catalog could be considered a "common service," particularly when it is thought about as a way of locating items through holdings lookup. The need for directory services (for data about policies, collections, rights, organizations, people) grows as we move towards a distributed environment. These are effectively "intelligence" that applications need to work smoothly and avoid redundant development effort. An example of such a directory is OCLC's ILL Policies Directory. Another is the "knowledge base" that is configured into current portal and resolver services. At the moment, each vendor or implementer creates a knowledge base with significant redundant cost. The knowledge base contains such data as descriptions of available resources, technical information about how to connect, and rights data. There is growing interest in making such data available nonredundantly as a "shared service." This idea makes technical sense, although it is not yet clear whether economic incentives exist to bring it about. "Registry" services typically allow applications to discover technical details that

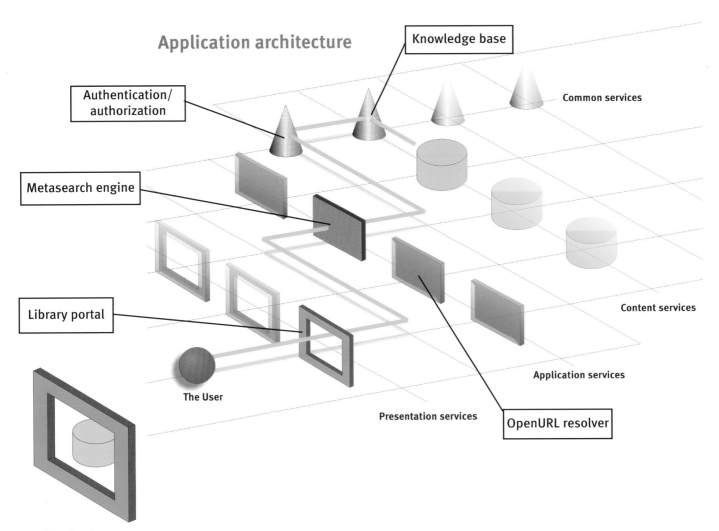

Application architecture

Knowledge base

Authentication/authorization

Metasearch engine

Library portal

The User

User's view

Common services

Content services

Application services

Presentation services

OpenURL resolver

are needed about registered entities. So, for example, OCLC runs a pilot OpenURL registry—this allows implementers of the new OpenURL specs to find authoritative data about identifiers and metadata schemas. Again, this type of application becomes more important as we move to distributed environments.

An example: Think about using a portal. Typically, the user will see a screen and can search several databases.

However, if we look "behind" or "through" the screen we see a potentially complex range of interactions. For example, consider a typical set of interactions to support a cross-searching application. The portal interface will give a view to the user of what is available. It will accept input and will pass to a metasearch engine. This in turn may need to look in a knowledge base to see how to interact with a particular resource. Authentication and authorization may be required at several stages. When some metadata is returned and the user selects an item it may be passed to an OpenURL resolver. This description simplifies the process, and there may be many other interactions. There may in fact be a range of other fine-grained services. Some metasearch engines merge and enhance metadata from third-party resources. Because of the heterogeneity of potential targets, there is a need for terminology services, where an application can interact with a service that maps vocabularies, expands searches and so on.

Say the item returned to the searcher of a portal was a book record and the user wants to initiate an interlibrary loan request. Then the portal might interact with a request broker service. It might have to select a library to send a request to based on a directory of rules, consult an ILL policy directory and send a request. It may have to interact with a common billing service.

It should be clear at this stage that this is an idealized schematic: in fact these systems are much more monolithic, enclosed and Tower-of-Babel-like than this representation suggests. However, the interconnected environment described in the last section suggests that there will have to be more decomposition of systems if we are to build flexible digital environments. This in turn suggests that we need effective and efficient links between the various components: they need to "click." This then raises the question of ensuring an appropriate standards framework to make this happen.

New standards

Repository and content standards

Consistent with the emergence of digital object management as a concern is a focus on standards to manage this emergence. Of special note are the following:

- **OAIS.** This provides a model for the development of archival repositories. It has provided a framework within which OCLC and others have developed their archives.

- **Preservation.** There is ongoing work on preservation metadata and exploratory work on how to actually provide preservation services. This area is still in early stages and there are serious issues for those aiming to provide production services.

- **Content packaging.** The library community has developed METS as a way of packaging complex digital objects for exchange and manipulation. The learning community has developed SCORM. Industry approaches such as MPEG 21 part 2 and SMIL may have some overlap also.

- **Content exchange.** We do not yet have a routinely implemented protocol framework for exchanging actual content between repositories. The work being carried out by the OKI initiative at MIT may be relevant here.

- **Metadata.** The metadata landscape continues to become more complex. Metadata is data that supports operations on objects. We have developed significant expertise in descriptive metadata for information objects. We now have new forms of metadata to support other operations. Some examples are: technical metadata (data about the technical characteristics of an object, what equipment was used to create it, etc.), structural metadata (metadata about the relations between components of an object), rights metadata. We also see metadata about other objects: collections, services, organizations, people. And finally, different domains and models are coming together in the shared space of the Web, so we need to work with schemas from related domains—ONIX (book industry), EAD (archives), IEEE/LOM (learning management) and so on.

Z39.50 International Maintenance Agency

www.loc.gov/z3950/agency

Applications

Application areas of note include:

- **Cross searching.** Z39.50 is a search and retrieve protocol that is widely adopted in the library and related communities for query. It is a complex protocol that is unlikely to grow in use. A parallel initiative is working on Z39.50 next generation: carrying Z39.50 over into a Web services environment. This work is resulting in two approaches SRW (search and retrieve on the Web) and SRU (search and retrieve URL). These are not widely adopted, but there is some expectation that they will be taken up in newer applications, and may find some traction outside the library community. They have been developed as "Web services."

Open Archives Initiative

www.openarchives.org

- **Harvesting.** There has been great interest in harvesting metadata, sparked by the Open Archives Initiative (OAI). An example here would be an OAI-PMH-based harvester that takes data from several sources and makes it available at a machine or a user interface. The Open Archives

NISO Standards Committee on OpenURL

www.niso.org/committees/
committee_ax.html

Initiative Protocol for Metadata Harvesting is a technique for sharing metadata between services. One service—a data provider in OAI terms—makes metadata available in an agreed way; another service comes and "harvests" it. The latter service—a service provider in OAI terms—may harvest from multiple "data providers" and in turn may provide access to the metadata it collects in this way.

- **Resolution.** A resolution service will typically take an identifier and return data about the resource identified. In the last couple of years a particular type of resolution service, based on the OpenURL, has become very important in library portal applications. An OpenURL provides a way of encoding citation data and exchanging it between services. Reference linking applications have emerged that are configured so as to resolve an OpenURL in a way that is configurable to the particular context of the user. So, in a typical scenario, given a journal article, a user might be directed to the local collection, to a particular aggregator and so on. This is a way of linking metadata for a resource with the "appropriate" copy of that resource, as determined by the library.

- **Niche library transaction applications.** NCIP and ISO ILL are two library-specific protocols. The latter is well established; the former is very recent. Neither is widely deployed, but each has a role in its niche area.

Universal access to information

Semantic Web, Web services, grid computing and wireless technology

Web Services and XML are related to business process management and people are recognizing that information is key in this.

Industry Pundit

"Well, there are a lot of problems with computing today, in how many things are still very manual or very isolated. You know, if you work with multiple PCs, phones and PDAs, the way you set up even trivial things like getting the sports scores that you care about, or the messages that are important, or your address book to be consistent on every device—that's a mess […] So, what's the key ingredient that can solve these problems? Well, it's largely about software breaking down boundaries. That's why our goal is to achieve what we call 'seamless computing'—between the structured and unstructured processes, between the devices, between the organizations."[19]

In common with other communities, the library community initially developed a range of domain-specific approaches. Also in common with other communities it is examining those approaches in the light of wider developments. Four are of special interest: the Semantic Web and Web services from the World Wide Web Consortium, grid computing and Wi-Fi. All of these, in one sense or another, attempt to address the less-than-seamless Internet-accessible world.

- **Semantic Web.** The objective of the semantic Web is to provide structure in Web documents, so that machines can process them in the way that people currently read them. So, at its core, the Semantic Web is about promoting languages for exchanging data and describing its meaning. Interoperability is enabled within a community, which uses a shared

19. Bill Schlender, "The Vision Thing Again," [interview with Bill Gates], *Business 2.0* (December 2003): 106.

"ontology" of terms. The general standard for data is the XML-based Resource Description Framework (RDF) and the upcoming Web Ontology Language (OWL).

The Semantic Web has yet to find convincing demonstrators, but may be important in niche applications. It is still largely theoretical. There is one area in which it is potentially important and this is in the area of terminology services. We are likely to see more vocabularies made available as network services. An example would be a network-accessible version of Dewey,® which could be queried, navigated and so on, by remote protocols. Work is underway on such applications, and there may be points of contact between these and the Semantic Web.

- **Web services.** Web services are of major significance for the library community and for applications builders in general. In brief, they allow lightweight applications to be defined, which leverages the existing infrastructure of the Web: they provide potentially low-barrier implementation routes for distributed services. Web services are modular applications available on the Web. They may be recombined to provide other services. Google and Amazon make interfaces available as Web services so that others can more easily build them into their applications. The Web services approach has wide uptake in industry. SRW/SRU protocols discussed above are rewrites of Z39.50 as Web services. OAI-PMH and OpenURLs are implemented as Web services. They are built on top of the Web, using basic Web protocols and XML.

- **Grid computing.** Grid computing (www.gridcomputing.com) promotes the development and advancement of technologies that provide seamless and scalable access to wide-area distributed resources. Computational grids enable the selection and sharing of geographically distributed computational resources. This idea is analogous to the electrical power grid, where power generators are distributed, but the users are able to access electric power without bothering about the source of energy and its location. The idea has become popular in a variety of academic research environments, including computer science, molecular modeling and drug design, biophysics and high-energy physics, and has been extended by IBM and others into business settings. The promise of grid computing—of Web-based services providing universal access to information and computing in a collaborative environment—is as real as it is seductive.[20]

- **Wireless technology.** Wi-Fi (wireless fidelity) refers to wireless local area networks that use one of several standards in the same "family"—the 802.11 standards. The wireless networks send and receive data to and from laptops and handheld devices such as cell phones, PDAs and the cell phone/PDA hybrids like the Treo. The resulting nomadic computing environment allows for flexibility, unencumbered by the need to locate wall plugs and hardwired computers. Many libraries are using Wi-Fi to deliver library content to users. Medical and health sciences libraries in particular are developing pathfinders and library information that can be downloaded to portable devices. Some libraries are using Wi-Fi and

There's a disconnect between libraries and consumer-oriented information management tools.

Industry Pundit

---

20. Willy Chui, "Grid Computing: Fulfilling the Promise of the Internet," *GridComputing Planet.com* (June 14, 2003), www.gridcomputingplanet.com/features/article.php/2234691.

handheld devices to collect data from copiers and printing stations, for example.

RFID (Radio Frequency Identification) is not a new wireless technology. What's new about RFID is that it has become cheap enough for large-scale deployment. Wal-Mart made the news this past year when they announced that they would require their 100 top suppliers to put RFID tags on pallets and cases of goods destined for Wal-Mart stores. Quite a few libraries have implemented RFID systems as a tool to help track materials, stop theft and check out and return books more rapidly. In a sense, RFID is the technological child of bar codes. The big difference between the bar codes and RFID tags are that bar codes have to be "seen" by a scanner and RFID tags can be read as long as they are within range of a reader. The difference to a library user may be the difference between standing in line waiting for access to a bar code scanner and having material checked out merely by entering the circulation area. One reason libraries have been slowly adopting RFID technology is cost, but as is always the case with technology, this inhibitor will eventually vanish. A more serious inhibitor is the concern many librarians have (and they have company in the Electronic Frontier Foundation) about the collection of data and individuals' privacy rights.

A 'Webby world'

The library world has been supported by some venerable applications: the MARC format, Z39.50 and others.

We have already discussed how new protocols are being developed in a Web services idiom. At the same time, metadata schema is being defined in an XML context.

Working collaboratively with people makes things happen.

Over the next few years, it is likely that most new protocol development will be in a Web services context. Modular applications will be quickly developed that advertise their interfaces for use by others.

Metadata and content standards will continue within a framework established by XML and the XML family of standards.

These developments will make library applications less specialized and domain-specific.

"I suppose you can say, 'Haven't we heard all this before? Didn't somebody talk about the digital convergence ten years ago? Didn't John Von Neumann have something to say about that in 1943?' Well, yes, but it has taken this long for a reason: It's hard."[21]

Here we chart the array of projects, technologies, standards and metadata initiatives, which are part of the library applications environment.

Libraries are used to handling semantically dense, richly structured data. A major challenge will be to handle more unstructured data. Libraries need to find ways of leveraging

21. Schlender, "Vision Thing."

their investment in structured approaches in relation to large amounts of unstructured materials on the Web that are being generated by research and learning activities.

Implications

- Many librarians and highly trained paraprofessionals will be retiring within the next five to ten years. *Is this "brain drain" a disaster or an opportunity?*

- Libraries and allied organizations increasingly have digital collections. *How are electronic collections to be defined and developed? Who owns digital information? How can its use be both protected and promoted?*

- The technical and economic challenges of digital preservation are significant and to some extent, still unknown. *Are archiving and preservation of all digital content possible? How should they be funded? Who decides what to archive and preserve?*

- Unmediated access to digital information is increasing. *How can the interpersonal aspects of librarianship—service, instruction, collaboration—be retained in a Webby world?*

- There is growing interest in providing integration—integration between information systems, and integration between information systems and other types of systems. *What is the function of the library in a networked distributed environment?*

What new attractions did we encounter on our tour through the Library Landscape? Perhaps not many. We know all the challenges, nightmares and dreams of this most familiar of landscapes. We read, write, speak and worry about them all. One thing is evident to anyone looking at the literature, published and unpublished, pertaining to the future of the library, or the future of the book, or the future of information professionals, in a digital world: it is often apocalyptic in one way or another. And we've been reading or writing it for at least ten years. It is possible to read an article published in 1992 on libraries in the digital age, substitute a few nouns and it's all timely and relevant in 2003. Granted, this tone is evident in library writing whatever year one picks to peruse—in the late 1800s, for example, fiction was going to ruin libraries. But, the point is, collectively, we do not seem to have made many of the changes to our landscape that the brightest among us have advocated for, on behalf of our larger communities.

This is not to suggest at all that libraries, allied organizations and companies serving these organizations have not made a huge number of changes to service delivery, information-seeking tools and products. At the risk of trivializing and over-simplifying decades of innovation, commitment and hard work, for the most part, what's been done has been done in a closed shop, using our own architects and consultants, with little direct assistance for our primary constituents, the information consumers. One result? Information Consumer is hanging out at the Information Mall with Google.

> *Bibliographic information is a corporate asset and should be treated like other assets.*
>
> Director, Academic Library

Future Frameworks

My Vision

To get to the library site,
type on the computer you're on,
in the address box at the top,
www.libraries.com

With a click of the mouse,
and a look at the screen,
all the libraries of Europe
can easily be seen.

Whether it's a story about the fairies glen,
or even ghosts and ghouls,
books from the past can be read with joy,
unless the readers are fools!

Libraries in the future can be on the net
on a special web-site address,
all the books and facts will be there,
and advice for bullying or distress.

The fact finder will be good for finding facts
the Second World War and more,
type in the facts you need to find
and you'll get more than you bargained for!

Or, if you want to get inspired,
why don't you sit and read a while,
and when you think you've read enough,
you can save your story on your file.

If you got stuck on your homework,
or if you want to do it there and then,
click on the homework help icon,
and you'll get ten out of ten!

If this work makes you hungry,
or you're thirsty for a drink,
because you're at home
you don't have to stop and think!

Words are a useful tool,
you can use them if you try,
so go to the dictionary or thesaurus site,
and you may find words that'll make you cry.

When you click on libraries of history
you can view libraries of old,
see how old the ancient books are
and see what secrets they unfold.

The smell of leather books of old,
in the future people will see,
crisp parchment and letters of gold,
written by monks in the tenth century.

View the furrowed pages,
and the writing advanced in years,
the words so strong can cause emotions,
laughter and some tears.

My library of the future,
will use technology,
to allow great books that are locked away
to be seen by you and me.

The great libraries of Alexandria,
and the monasteries of Rome,
will reveal hidden treasures,
in the comfort of your home.

For each book will be scanned,
electronically of course,
and a hologram created,
it's the new modern force!

The holograms are easily viewed,
across the Internet,
just log onto libraries of the world
and within a minute you'll be met.

Choose any library of interest to you,
any book, no matter how rare,
and with a tiny click of the mouse,
the hologram will be there.

You can marvel at the colours,
and the details in the book,
you will be so inspired,
you'll take another look.

All this can come true,
but not in the century we're in,
so maybe this library I created will be real,
let the future begin!

By Kirstie
Weatherhead High School
United Kingdom[1]

1. Year 7 student at Weatherhead High School in the UK, www.weatherhead.wirral.sch.uk/news/poems.htm#poem4.

What patterns were discerned in the tour through the twilight zone? We have identified trends in five landscapes and set out implications that seem to be significant to each landscape. There may be few that surprise readers but the purpose of this scan is not to unravel the fabric of the whole information world and reweave it into a new pattern, presented as whole cloth. The purpose is to surface trends and issues that, told as a whole story, might lead us to notice some aspect of a familiar trend, that when juxtaposed with another trend, exposes a pattern we did not notice before. "What haven't you noticed lately?"

For the OCLC staff compiling this report, many trends were thought-provoking and informative. Three patterns in the fabric of information and knowledge management stand out among many. One might be described as a decrease (or disappearance in some cases) in guided access to content. The second pattern is perhaps an element of the first: there is a trend to disaggregation not just of content, but also of services, technology, economics and institutions. The third pattern is that of collaboration: gaming, open-source software, Web conferencing, blogs, instant messaging, learning objects and "hack fests" are all forms of collaboration, enabled by advances in technology. The three trends have deep implications for all the organizational areas of libraries and allied organizations.

Pattern one: decrease in guided access to content

Guided access to content refers not only to humans acting as intermediaries between consumer and information object, but also to the containers of information—databases, reference books and library catalogs.

Human guides to content are librarians and teachers, but they are also bank tellers and doctors. All of these people mediate between the enquirer and the information: they interpret information into knowledge. "How much interest did I earn last quarter?" "What are the symptoms of a heart attack?" "Why is the sky blue?" "I need to find three articles analyzing the significance of birds in Shakespeare's plays." In the past, teachers, bank tellers and doctors synthesized and interpreted on behalf of enquirers who were, for a number of reasons, unable to get at the information themselves. Much of that specialized, proprietary information may still be under the control of the human guide but some of it is not, and it has made its way to the Web to be joined by literally millions of pages of content that is searchable, findable and usable without assistance from human guides.

In a physical world, the actual containers of information themselves guide users. A book, by its shape and size, by its cover and even price, alerts the reader to what might be inside. A popular magazine is easily identified by its glossy appearance and many photographs. No information consumer is going to accidentally pick up a copy of the academic journal *Brain Research* when it was *Entertainment Weekly* he wanted. To some extent, the "shapes" of the containers of information have been retained in a virtual world: e-journal pages look just like their print ones, a record in a library catalog or in WorldCat still looks much like the catalog card. But in a world where information and content increasingly are unbound from containers, the containers cannot act as guides.

"The needs of the library user are the most important consideration. Thus, for planning purposes, it is necessary to ask what are the user's needs and how are they changing. This, then, provides a context for reconsidering library services and collections."[2]

2.   Gregg Sapp and Ron Gilmour, "A Brief History of the Future of Academic Libraries," *Libraries and the Academy* (2003): 16.

Research

self-sufficient

OCLC

lifelong learning

funding

Social

*Information Consumer
is comfortable
traveling alone.*

As a result, the information consumer operates in an increasingly autonomous way and is frequently self-sufficient, choosing simple searches and search interfaces over complex ones.

Google and Amazon both offer very simple search interfaces. Google, in particular, relies on its search technology to deliver meaningful results, instead of searcher's knowledge of the search indices. Librarians and information professionals have had ample evidence for years that most searchers use a single term when searching—regardless of the sophistication of the interface. Why, then, do most library content interfaces still contain multiple search boxes? In one sense, the complex presentation is an attempt to guide searchers as they seek information, guaranteeing better search results if the guide is "consulted." In the "Webby world" described in this report, more and more people do not seek out a mediator in their quest for knowledge, and are happy to pursue their information quest unattended by a guide.[3]

Even if Information Consumer wanted a guide, there are few available.

Libraries and aggregators of content have not capitalized on the chance to "lurk" alongside the information seeker in a seamless Web environment, and appear as an advisor and guide when searching is unsuccessful. "The key is to always be next to the user wherever the user is, invisible when things are working, magically materializing when they are not."[4] At the moment, the information consumer must make the choice to go to an "ask-a" service, or to a virtual reference service offered through a library to seek advice on the Web. The searcher must also come to the service, rather than the librarian coming to the user. No icon exists to add to a browser tool bar that will invoke a wise advisor.

It is human nature to seek information and advice as close to oneself as possible. This advice may live within a circle of family and friends, a personal library, and other reliable "close" resources, such as the Google search box that is so conveniently located on many browser tool bars. "There is a lot of groundwork libraries can lay that would be invisible, and we can stand at the ready as a trust circle when further service is needed. The unanswered question is how to move our circle closer, in a person's network, at the level of *their* need."[5]

Pattern two: disaggregation
The second pattern to emerge from the twilight is the rapid and widespread reduction of content and institutions to much smaller units of use and interaction than in the past.

Librarians and publishers are familiar with the term "the least publishable unit," which referred to e-journal articles at the time they came into vogue. Now, "microcontent" is generally used to describe even smaller units of content that come from some larger whole.

---

3. One interesting aspect of this is that information consumers seem to be quite comfortable using primary material—reading the digitized letters of George Washington Carver, for example, rather than a book about the letters—if that material is available.
4. Jenny Levine, e-mail, December 5, 2003.
5. Ibid.

As e-journals proliferated, people realized it should no longer be necessary to purchase the entire journal if only one article was required. So, the journal as a definable unit became less important. As more and more content made its way to the Web, the granularity of the least publishable unit increased. It is possible and often even easy to locate a table, a fact, a quote, a picture and single song from what used to be aggregated, monolithic content: books, journal articles, government reports, records and CDs. Increasingly, the information seeker doesn't care what the original container looked like, and wants to be able to use this microcontent immediately. The information is fungible and the boundaries of the containers fade and blur. Content is disaggregated from its original container. Amazon's "search inside" ups the ante in this arena, raising consumer expectations that content is searchable and definable at a micro level, and, we predict, payable for—at the micro level. Micropayment for microcontent is the next logical step.

Institutions and services, and the technologies that enable them, are increasingly disaggregated. E-learning disaggregates the learning process from the institution as students avail themselves of the "least unit": a course can possibly be independent of place and time—tied to the parent institution in name only. Banking online reduces "the bank" to a series of activities, and the ordered presentation of a library's physical collection of content and its highly structured services can be irrelevant and even inhibitory in a digital world. A nine-year-old's Web page about spiders coexists with a presentation at a conference by the world's expert on spiders and may be deemed more useful to a nine-year-old searcher than the expert's paper. It's about more than just content. It's about context. We'll return to this notion of context: it's really important.

Pattern three: collaboration

In a whole variety of ways, using all sorts of technology, it really is becoming easier for people to connect to do things together. The pattern that clearly emerged as we scanned the landscapes is that the technology adoption curve is very fast for devices and environments that allow people to work together and talk to one another seamlessly—untethered from classrooms, labs, electrical outlets and time. The desire for better collaborative tools, software and environments, however, is not new. Michael Schrage wrote *Shared Minds: The New Technologies of Collaboration* in 1990 about the technologies on the horizon that promised to encourage and foster collaboration. Almost 15 years later, we might all truly be poised to reap the benefits of collaboration technologies. Bill Gates believes that the next great leap forward in computing terms will engineer social change as barriers among people, systems and information disappear. He touts "Longhorn," the next edition of Windows, as a collaboration framework, rather than a computing platform.[6]

Perhaps it's time to coin a new term to use in a seamless computing environment. Rather than "connect" or be "connected," people will "context"

Technology

context

Economic

"social" software

collaboration

Library

Librarians have always excelled at providing context.

6.   "Bill Gates at COMDEX 2003: The Era of Seamless Computing," *PressPass* (November 16, 2003), www.microsoft.com/billgates/.

or be "contexted." In an infosphere that continues to get larger and more diverse, context will be ever more important. As we've discussed above, the people and institutions that acted as guides to content disappeared into a virtual world and have not been replaced in any meaningful way.

Librarians have always excelled at providing context. Amazon and others work to emulate this role by building context into personalization systems and other collaborative technologies. Amazon has, in essence, built a readers' advisory service into its Web site. "People who read this book also liked these titles." The service that librarians offered to readers in a pre-Internet, face-to-face world has not been translated into the catalog or library Web site environments. There are many readers' advisory Web sites, but they offer no personalization features or advisory technology beyond lists of titles organized in various ways. Context is not there. Amazon currently fills a void. Privacy issues in an online environment might have prevented librarians from acting on the need people have for context. What is clear from the trends scanned is that people hunger for context and environments that encourage dialogue, conversation and the ability to share. Librarians by nature will welcome virtual work environments that encourage dialogue, conversation and the ability to share and collaborate with colleagues and with information consumers.

It is important to note that a search for content and context in the infosphere may not yet reveal libraries and their sister organizations. But a visit to a physical library—particularly a public library—will reveal a place that is full of people seeking content and context. As we observed in the *Research and Learning Landscape,* libraries are places of social assembly and are vitally important to their communities.

Future frameworks

What might these three patterns suggest for the future of libraries, allied organizations and the companies that serve them? We will argue that the only way to answer this question is to re-view the landscape using the lens of the information consumer.

How does a library appear today through the information consumer's lens? What is the shape of the user's "infosphere?" The following diagram suggests how the information grid of material might look when viewed from the user's perspective.[8]

How do the users view the library in their personal infosphere? The library is in focus when a book is needed or if attempts to find the materials on the Web are unsuccessful. But just how much mind share the library holds is fuzzy, based on the patterns surfaced in this report. And perhaps, the goal of libraries might be invisibility, in the sense that the service is ubiquitous and fully integrated in the infosphere—to be in the circle next to the user.

"Human systems need inputs of human energy to do well. Everything else— the Internet, agents, wireless, knowledge-mining—is contingent. They're support, not the thing itself."[7]

---

7. John Thackara, "The Thermodynamics of Cooperation," In *The Bubble* [online magazine] (September 2003): n.p. From Doors of Perception: www.doorsofperception.com.
8. Based on the *Collections Grid* that was used to frame the interviews done for this report.

After all, technology and services are most welcome in our lives when we do not have to devote much thought to them. We press a switch and light comes or goes. Expecting the information consumer to pay attention to the differences between William Shakespeare the author and William Shakespeare the subject as search terms is akin to expecting Joe Householder to know if the red wire or the black wire should be grounded before he plugs the lamp in—and to expect Joe to go to RedWire.com to figure out what happens if he's wrong. Thankfully, clever people have hidden all this technology inside a box and millions are saved from a shocking experience.

What might the trends presented in this scan suggest for OCLC and other organizations working with libraries to deliver services and products to information consumers?

Some questions arise: Is there a future for the proprietary containers built to guide access to content? If content is increasingly sought after in a "least publishable unit," does it make sense to devote many resources to building containers? If so, what should the mechanisms of mediation be, and are these being developed? Can OCLC disaggregate itself and its services in order to meet the needs of self-service consumers interested in microcontent? And how can OCLC and others link the worlds of order and chaos, and empower the information consumer to be well-guided? OCLC members and participants value structure and mediated content. Evidence suggests that libraries' constituents do not value these elements to the same degree. Who then—which constituents—should OCLC research when building a product and service strategy? How can OCLC and other organizations collaborate with libraries to effect changes that bring the collective wealth of libraries to the attention and desktop of the information consumer?

The challenges inherent in such changes should not be viewed as threatening but as an opportunity for renewal and rejuvenation. But how do we decide what to do? Libraries and museums in particular have introduced new services and programs, built up over the old ones in almost archaeological layers. But preservation of everything is an unaffordable luxury. We have to embrace the opportunity of the changed landscape, not reconstitute the old landscape in a new space.

"It is almost impossible to achieve the requisite awareness of what we haven't noticed while we are immersed in a nice, comfortable, or at least accustomed environment. We are all subject to the ground rules, that is, the rules and unperceived effects that govern our business ground or context. It is like asking a fish to suddenly become aware of water. [Marshall] McLuhan observed, 'One thing about which fish know exactly nothing is water, since they have no anti-environment which would enable them to perceive the element they live in.' It is only when it is pulled from the water that

A user's view of the "infosphere"

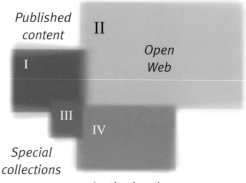

Published content — II — *Open Web* — I — III — IV — *Special collections* — *Institutional content*

Libraries' space within the user's "infosphere"

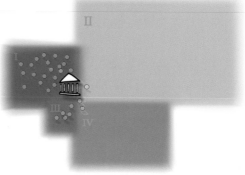

"We have to preserve the identities and reputations we have built in our communities—while morphing into entities that are very different."[9]

the fish becomes acutely aware of its former environment. The challenge in achieving awareness to notice the formerly unnoticed—what we call 'integral awareness' of our total business environment—is to create an appropriate anti-environment."[10]

The anti-environment. What if libraries and OCLC and all the other players in the world of structured access to information erased the organizational charts, the artificial separations of content, the visible taxonomies, and the other edifices real or otherwise built to bring order and rationality to what we perceive as a chaotic universe? What if we built an infosphere rich in content and context that was easy to use, ubiquitous and integrated, designed to become woven into the fabric of people's lives; people looking for answers, meaning and authoritative, trustable results? How do we take information, information sources and our expertise to the user, rather than making the user come to our spheres?

If all the trends in this environmental scan were distilled into one statement it might look something like this (incredibly obvious) truism: **Libraries and allied organizations do not exist separately from their communities**.

There's a perhaps apocryphal business school example that is instructive here. When Joe Householder goes to a hardware store to buy a drill, he's not actually buying a drill. He's buying the ability to make a small hole. Perhaps libraries and allied organizations have become overly focused on drills of late.

In 1971, Fred Kilgour built a really good drill, better than any others that were made around then, and he got it to the marketplace before other good drills were built. That drill is WorldCat. But, the power of the Kilgour drill was not that the drill bit was more robust than others, or that the motor was larger. It was that a good tool gave people a better way of doing things—specifically cataloging things other people had already cataloged. And that is a very good and powerful model. It saved people and institutions time, and allowed, for the first time, a way of seeing what other libraries had in their collections. A technological innovation became a collaborative revolution. With WorldCat as the "metadata hub," OCLC has been able to broaden the scope of its services over the years, helping libraries serve Information Consumer. How do we together build on this remarkable legacy to capitalize on collaboration technologies, push technologies, personalization, open-source software, gaming and the energy of young information professionals—and take our world to Information Consumer's world?

Coming together as community

There are so many interesting challenges inherent in our landscape that it is not surprising that we have become fragmented as a community: there's something there to interest everyone. But, it is time to put individual interests aside and come together as a community to reestablish our

9. Robert Coonrod, "Creating the Digital Future," *First Monday* 8, no. 5 (May 2003): n.p., www.firstmonday.dk/issues/issues8_5/index.html.
10. Mark Federman, "Enterprise Awareness McLuhan Thinking," Keynote speech at the *Information Highways* conference, Toronto, Canada (March 25, 2003): 4.

preeminence in search and retrieval, information and knowledge management, metadata creation and collaboration. Libraries are exemplars of the notion that the whole is greater than the sum of its parts. Collaboration has built the foundations of modern librarianship and must form the foundation of the new "infosphere" in which libraries and allied organizations marry technology with collaboration to deliver services to the information consumer.

Libraries, museums, historical societies and information industry companies are filled with very bright, dedicated people who sit on committees, attend conferences, deliver papers and, perhaps, now and then, wake up at 3 am wondering, so, what is the future of libraries, of my museum? One trend that was evident in this scan was that for at least ten years, all those bright people have been writing and speaking eloquently about possible futures. Yet, not much has fundamentally changed. Rather than dissect why this might be so, here's a proposal.

The library community could hold a "hackfest,"[11] an agenda-less conference that identified a set of problems that needed fixing and then let loose clever people to come up with solutions. "Get a bunch of smart and capable people in a room with the time allocated to focus on a problem or a set of problems, and magic can happen."[12] Some of those clever people would have to be information consumers, young and old, so that solutions were designed *with* them, not *for* them. "We guess at how to do this quite a bit, but I don't think we actually study these issues outside of the library world, which is where it is more important to be these days. In a way, that's the 'anti-environment.' We already have a lot of research explaining how users fit into our infosphere. Now, we need to start with bleeding edge adopters, all the way down to those most left behind by the digital divide (by necessity or by choice) and follow them around, ask questions, observe them to find out how libraries and our services fit into their worlds. It's a very key difference and you'd have to start with no existing assumptions of how library services already reach these people, which can be very difficult to do."[13]

Let the future begin

There are, of course, many more implications inherent in this environment than only those suggested in this scan. Many trends have not been noted, and just about all specific products and services that libraries, allied organizations and companies offer have been left out. And there are many more questions that arise than are expressed here.

Many readers are familiar with Douglas Adams's *Hitchhiker's Guide to the Universe* and subsequent works. It seems relevant to end this environmental

Potential role of libraries in the "infosphere"

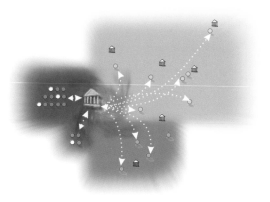

Libraries are exemplars of the notion that the whole is greater than the sum of its parts.

11. Roy Tennant reported in the November 15, 2003 *Library Journal* on the energy and success of the HackFest that took place in 2002–2003 at Access conferences.
12. Roy Tennant, e-mail, December 2, 2003.
13. Jenny Levine, e-mail, December 10, 2003.

scan with a reminder that asking the right question is more important than asking a lot of questions.

"The answer to the Ultimate Question of Life, the Universe and Everything—as given by the supercomputer Deep Thought to a group of mice in Douglas Adams's comic science fiction series *The Hitchhiker's Guide to the Galaxy*—is 42. According to the *Guide,* mice are 3-dimensional profiles of a pan-dimensional, super-intelligent race of beings. They built Deep Thought, the second greatest computer of all time and space, to tell them the answer to the question of life, the universe and everything. After seven and a half million years the computer divulges the answer: 42.

'Forty-two!' yelled Loonquawl. 'Is that all you've got to show for seven and a half million years' work?'

'I checked it very thoroughly, said the computer, and that quite definitely is the answer. I think the problem, to be quite honest with you, is that you've never actually known what the question is.'"[14]

Information on the Web is fragmented; disaggregation of content splinters it further. Seamless computing may expose even more content to Information Consumer. Few institutions outside of libraries have the ability to put the pieces of the puzzle back together or build the trails for navigation, but it is critical that the right questions are asked.[15]

The question is not what should be digitized and preserved. The question is not what role will the library play in the institutional repository. The question is not MARC or METS or MODS. The question is not how will retiring librarians be replaced. The critical question is how does Fazeela in the Maldives complete her school assignment on wolf snakes? How does Adrian in England finish his family tree? How can Kofi in Ghana find scientific data on mercury levels in Volta Lake?

The ultimate question of life, the universe and everything is: How do we together, as a community of libraries and allied organizations, move our trusted circle closer to information consumers at the level of *their* need?

OCLC wants to hear from you. Each landscape ended with a set of implications we think are apparent from scanning the environment, as well as a set of questions that arise from those implications. Please answer these questions. Ask others. Suggest solutions.

The Web version of this report is available at **www.oclc.org/membership/escan/** and you can send us your comments from there. You can also send e-mail to **escan@oclc.org** or send mail to **Environmental Scan, OCLC, MC 235, 6565 Frantz Road, Dublin OH, USA 43017-3395**.

Help OCLC recognize patterns in our shared landscape.

All this can come true...

so maybe this library I created will be real,

let the future begin!

Kirstie

14. Wikipedia, the free encyclopedia, www.wikipedia.org/wiki/The_Answer_to_Life,_the_Universe,_and_Everything.
15. Jenny Levine, e-mail, December 4, 2003.

Appendices

Page

109   OCLC

113   Glossary

125   Collections Grid

127   People Consulted

133   Readings & Sources

149   Notes & Ideas

OCLC

OCLC Online Computer Library Center, Inc. is a nonprofit organization, established in Ohio in 1967 by a small group of libraries whose leaders believed that working together they could find practical solutions to some of the day's most challenging issues. What began as a "challenge to use newly available computer technology to automate the traditional library card catalog" rapidly became a collaborative revolution that involved thousands of libraries around the world. Working together, libraries in the OCLC cooperative created the "world's library catalog," WorldCat®.

Today, WorldCat is the world's largest library information resource, containing more than 900 million library records, and covering more than 50 million unique items. Every day, librarians from across the globe enrich WorldCat by adding critical metadata and data about books, maps, Web sites, DVDs, musical scores and other artifacts of human effort, as well as links to Web-based resources such as e-journals, e-books and photographs. WorldCat makes it possible for information consumers and librarians to conduct 100 million searches and view 15 million articles online each year.

Collaboration among librarians and OCLC solved the practical problem of automating cataloging. Ongoing collaboration led to a broad range of additional solutions for libraries. The OCLC membership jointly created the largest interlibrary loan system in the world, delivering more than 9 million items annually to information consumers across the globe. In 2001, the OCLC cooperative began initiatives to deliver innovative services that will enable libraries to increase access to and better preserve the growing world of digital content.

In addition to the many services offered, the OCLC cooperative also funds a very active research program that recently celebrated 25 years of innovation and service to the worldwide library community. OCLC Research incubates new technologies, sponsors the work of library scientists and serves on global standards bodies. In addition to advancing information access and exchange standards, OCLC Research is also actively engaged with the world's information community to further the science of librarianship.

The trends uncovered in *The 2003 OCLC Environmental Scan,* the feedback and recommendations that will be gathered from OCLC members, and the information community's response to these materials will help shape future initiatives, activities and services of the cooperative. Some "future forward" initiatives are already underway.

Current OCLC initiatives

OCLC and its member libraries are involved in many initiatives and programs that reflect several of the trends identified in the scan. Among these programs are:

Web access to the world's catalog—WorldCat. Working with libraries, information partners and search engine providers, OCLC is working to bring WorldCat directly to the Information Consumer. An information seeker who starts a search using a search engine could, in the near future, discover the items or information needed at a nearby library.
www.oclc.org/worldcat/pilot/

Open-source software. The world is quickly discovering what the library and information community has known for years—information without metadata is nearly unusable in this electronic information environment. OCLC Research sponsors many open-source initiatives and provides open-source tools that can broaden the use of metadata.

- **FRBR.** This open-source software application simplifies searching and retrieval for information seekers by restructuring library catalogs. Rather than seeing multiple records for what looks like the same intellectual content, the searcher will see a single record representing various intellectual or artistic realizations of a work.
  www.oclc.org/research/projects/frbr/

- **OAICat.** This open-source software application makes metadata from a database, archive or repository available for harvesting via the Open Archives Initiative Protocol for Metadata Harvesting (OAI-PMH). OAICat increases the visibility of institutions' resources by making it easy to distribute metadata to a wide audience of users.
  www.oclc.org/research/software/oai/cat.htm

- **OAIHarvester.** This open-source software application automatically harvests metadata from databases, archives or repositories that are compliant with the Open Archives Initiative Protocol for Metadata Harvesting (OAI-PMH). OAIHarvester makes it easy for institutions to collect metadata from a wide variety of data providers and thus build their own services to provide access to the described resources.
  www.oclc.org/research/software/oai/harvester2.htm

For more information about OCLC open-source initiatives, see:
www.oclc.org/research/software/

E-learning. The OCLC E-learning Task force, composed of librarians, administrators, faculty and instructional technologists, is exploring the roles libraries might play in the e-learning landscape. E-learning includes distance learning, online learning and electronic elements incorporated into traditional teaching and learning processes.
www.oclc.org/info/elearning/

Standards and activities. The OCLC cooperative represents libraries in a range of standards and professional communities, including: Dublin Core Metadata Initiative, Open Archives Initiative, American Library Association, the National Information Standards Organization, the Center for Research Libraries and the International Federation of Library Associations and Institutions.

Other information resources. In addition to this environmental scan, OCLC develops studies and other information sources that OCLC members use in their planning and in their own advocacy activities. A few of the latest studies and programs include:

- *Five-Year Information Format Trends.* The OCLC Library & Information Center compiled this report, which outlines trends in popular and scholarly materials, digitization projects and Web resources.
  www.oclc.org/info/trends/

- *The Incentives to Preserve Digital Materials: Roles, Scenarios, and Economic Decision-Making.* This white paper explores the economics of digital preservation.
  www.oclc.org/research/projects/digipres/incentives-dp.pdf

- *Libraries: How they stack up.* This report compares library economics and activities to other sectors, professions and destinations in the worldwide economy.
  www.oclc.org/info/compare/

- *OCLC Library Training & Education Market Needs Assessment Study.* This report defines the training and continuing education needs of library workers and identifies how OCLC might help serve those needs through online training offerings.
  www.oclc.org/info/needsassessment/

To learn more about OCLC and the OCLC cooperative, visit **www.oclc.org**.

Glossary

Application sharing—A feature of many videoconferencing applications that enables the conference participants to simultaneously run the same application. The application itself resides on only one of the machines connected to the conference.

Asset management (e.g., DSpace)—Used here to refer to the activities required to build and maintain digital collections to capture and preserve the intellectual output of a single- or multiuniversity community and/or academic discipline. See also "Institutional repository."

Audio conferencing—The process of conducting a conference between two or more participants in such a way that only the voices of the participants are heard.

Auto-classification—An automated, computerized process to sort items into a taxonomical system, such as matching numbers in the Dewey Decimal Classification system to book titles.

Automatic taxonomy creation—Generation of a taxonomy structure by parsing a document's keyword phrase distributions.

Automatic text categorization—Uses statistical models or hard-coded rules to rate a document's relevancy to certain subject categories, which helps organize information better by grouping similar subjects together while separating dissimilar texts.

Autonomous systems—Systems that solve problems or robustly maintain a level of functionality while limiting human intervention. Typically based on rules and statistical methods that have been developed for artificial intelligence.

Bandwidth—A measure of capacity in a channel for electronic communication. Bandwidth is often expressed by users as a measurement of speed. The higher the bandwidth, the less time it takes to transmit information.

Blog (or **Web log**)—A Web-based journal of short, dated entries in reverse chronological order. Most blogs focus on one subject area and are updated daily. Entries typically consist of links to external Web pages with summaries of or commentary on the content. See also "Corporate blogging."

BPM (Business process management)—The process of integrating and managing an enterprise's processes for efficiency and effectiveness.

Bulletin board—A bulletin board functions very much like a newsgroup with the users of the board posting messages; these messages are then displayed to all those who access the bulletin board. It is a low-tech solution for providing a forum for users whose numbers are too small or whose focus of interest is too specialized to be supported by a newsgroup.

Chat—The process of communicating with other Internet users in real time.

Commercial grids—Grids formed for nonscientific, nontechnical tasks across multiple enterprises to address a single, large-scale purpose. Grids can also be used within one enterprise. The term "grid" is sometimes misused to denote the related technologies of distributed and utility computing.

Competitive intelligence—The analysis of an enterprise's business environment.

Consumer digital rights management—Consumer-oriented protection from misuse of copyright of intellectual property, distributed in digital form.

Content aggregation and syndication—Aggregation allows content from multiple sources to be consolidated into one repository or Web site. Syndication allows desired content to be distributed between servers efficiently.

Content aggregator—An individual or organization that amasses or collects information for resale.

Content integration—Tools to link the content that is dispersed throughout the enterprise in diverse applications and databases.

Corporate blogging—The application of personal online publishing "Web log" styles—that is, online publishing in a daily or frequently updated "log" format—to corporate objectives.

CRM (Customer relationship management)—A system for managing and integrating all of an enterprise's interactions with customers to provide consistency and effectiveness.

Data mining—Transforming raw data into higher-level constructs, such as predictive models, explanatory models, filters or summaries by using algorithms from fields such as artificial intelligence and statistics. Techniques used can range from very simple models, such as arithmetic averages; those of intermediate complexity, for example, linear regression, clustering, decision trees, case-based reasoning and k-nearest neighbor; to very complicated models including neural networks and Bayesian networks.

Desktop sharing—Using conferencing technology to enable multiple users to see one computer desktop, often used for product demonstrations.

Dewey Decimal Classification—A general knowledge organization tool owned by OCLC Online Computer Library Center that is continuously revised to keep pace with knowledge. www.oclc.org/dewey

Digital asset management—Provides a repository for data types such as images, audio and video. Functionality should include search and manipulation of these objects.

Digital divide—A metaphorical description of the boundary between people affluent enough to have a personal computer regularly at their disposal and those who can not.

Digital Rights Management (DRM)—Technology or technologies that enable the secure distribution, promotion and sale of digital media content.

Disintermediation—Occurs when simplifications in technology, economic forces or other causes displace someone, usually an intermediary, from a customary role in a process. This term is also used as a verb to describe how this displacement process happens; for example, computerized typesetting systems in the newspaper companies disintermediated the linotype machines; operators who were their predecessors a few generations earlier disintermediated manual typesetters.

Disruptive technologies—New products or distribution processes superior to the ones they replace. They characteristically simplify those processes, improve the product and reduce costs so much that they change the basis of competition in an entire industry. Disruptive technologies typically destroy companies and even whole industries. The eventual disruption of the integrated steel producing companies by the minimills is the historical process that gave rise to this concept.

Document exchange—The sharing of documents over the Internet.

Document imaging—A mature technology for rendering paper documents as electronic images.

Document management—A server-based repository that offers library services at a minimum, with many extended and related technologies.

Document visualization—Display of two-dimensional maps that place similar documents together.

DOI (Digital Object Identifiers)—System for identifying and exchanging intellectual property in the digital environment. It allows for the construction of automated services and transactions for e-commerce. www.doi.org

Dublin Core—The outcome of a workshop held in 1995 by OCLC and the National Center for Supercomputing Applications (NCSA) at which the participants explored simpler ways of describing the wide variety of resources held by various organizations including libraries, museums, archives, governments and publishers. Participants proposed a core set of metadata elements for describing Web-based resources for easier search and retrieval. The resulting Dublin Core is a 15-element set intended to emphasize retrieval, as described above, rather than description. It facilitates discovery of electronic resources and enables interoperability between metadata repositories. http://dublincore.org

EAD (Encoded Archival Description)—A standard for encoding archival finding aids using the Standard Generalized Markup Language (SGML).

E-book readers—Handheld digital devices to store and display text. Most can store many books and have backlit screens and adjustable fonts.

E-books (content)—Books, including textbooks, fiction, nonfiction consumer and educational, made available digitally and electronically rather than by codex. This includes text that has been converted from print to digital form, digital images and digital audio books, as well as content that was "born digital."

ebXML—A family of commercial standards, including ebXML Collaboration Protocol Profile and Agreement, ebXML Implement, ebXML Messaging and ebXML Registry, designed to provide for common formats and processes for conducting collaborative commerce. http://ebxml.org

E-Commerce—The general exchange of goods and services electronically. E-commerce can occur between users and vendors, or business-to-business (B2B) through electronic data interchange (EDI).

Economies of scale—Economies based on the principle that the more you produce of any item, the less cost of each item. This principle is apparent especially in mechanized and automated-production processes. Unit costs usually decrease when volumes increase for many reasons, ranging from enhanced worker skill to price savings in the purchase of raw materials.

E-journals—Journals, magazines, e-zines, webzines, newsletters and types of serial publications that are available electronically.

E-learning—The use of electronic technologies to deliver cognitive information and training that improves understanding and competency.

E-mail—A form of electronic messaging where a user creates a text message (that may have a number of attachments) and sends it to a recipient.

Enabling technology—A technology that enables or drives changes in any number of downstream phenomena: product cost, user expectations, product quality, etc.

Expertise location and management—A tacit knowledge capture and sharing process supported by dynamic profiling technologies and workflow.

Extended enterprise—A term used to denote a company and the partners and allies with which it works very closely. It can appear as though they collectively constitute a single enterprise.

External Web services deployments—The use of Web services to provide enterprises with data interchange and noninvasive application integration.

FRBR (Functional Requirements for Bibliographic Records)—A 1998 recommendation of the International Federation of Library Associations and Institutions (IFLA) to restructure catalog databases to reflect the conceptual structure of information resources. The FRBR model includes four levels of representation: work, expression, manifestation and item.

Future-state vision—An encompassing term for many future aspects of an organization, such as the purpose of the organization; what it wants to accomplish; how it wishes others to perceive it; strategies for carrying out work (and the rationales behind them); organizational premises, objectives, culture and common values.

Grid computing—A form of networking. Unlike conventional networks that focus on communication among devices, grid computing harnesses unused processing cycles of all computers in a network for solving problems too intensive for any stand-alone machine. Grid computing requires special software that is unique to the computing project for which the grid is being used. www.gridcomputing.com

Idea management—A process for developing, identifying and using valuable insights or alternatives that would otherwise not have emerged.

Identity Management—A broad administrative area that deals with identifying individuals in a system (a network, a country, an enterprise) and controlling their access to resources within that system by associating user rights and restrictions with the established identity.

ILL (Interlibrary Loan)—A protocol that establishes a messaging framework for borrowing and lending transactions between libraries.

IM (Instant messaging)—The generic name of a technology that enables private chat to take place. When the user of this technology logs in to the Internet he or she will be informed which correspondents are online. They also receive any messages their friends have left for them and they can then interact with their friends using online chat.

Information extraction—Culls concepts, such as names, geographic entities and relationships, from unstructured data (mostly text).

Information literacy—The skills required to use the search-and-find technologies to locate and sift through information as well as the skills needed to use that information effectively.

Information quality—A characteristic that establishes the relevance, reliability and other attributes that make information suitable to support knowledge work, decision-making and legal reporting requirements.

Information retrieval/search—The retrieval of documents based on a similarity metric applied to a user's query.

Institutional repository—Digital collections that capture and preserve the intellectual output of a single- or multiuniversity community.

Intelligent agents—Software that exhibits a large degree of autonomy, decentralized authority and robustness in dynamically changing environments.

Internal Web services—The use of Web services inside enterprise security perimeters to accomplish noninvasive integration.

ISO ILL—An international standard for conducting interlibrary loans between systems.

J2EE (Java 2, Enterprise Edition)—Widely-used platform for building, deploying and managing Web services.

LCSH—Library of Congress Subject Headings.

Learning object—A mixture of content, assessment and learning outcomes that are tightly bound for a particular learning topic and can be repurposed.

Library Web services—Web services that enable the sharing of library resources among users.

Location-aware services—Cellular network technology to provide services that are relevant to a specific user location, e.g., safety, information and tracking.

LOM (Learning Object Metadata)—Metadata specification for describing learning objects, defined here as any entity, digital or nondigital, that can be used, reused or referenced during technology-supported learning.

MARC21—Machine Readable Cataloging standard.

Mass customization—Mass customization is to be distinguished from mass production. Mass production follows the "one-size-fits-all" model. Unique customer needs are more or less ignored. Mass customization implies more advanced management and marketing techniques for ordering, manufacturing and delivering relatively customized products to unique customer segments. Mass customization meets and satisfies special needs much better by delivering relatively customized products to common-interest customer groups.

METS (Metadata Encoding and Transmission Standard)—Standard for encoding descriptive, administrative and structural metadata regarding objects within a digital library, expressed using the XML schema language.

Mind share—A market research term. If a product or brand name is so completely familiar that most members of a defined population instantly recall it when stimulated by associated ideas, text, product or brand, this product or name is said to have mind share.

MODS (Metadata Object Description Scheme)—Could be called "MARC Lite." A bibliographic element set that may be used for a variety of purposes, and particularly for library applications. It includes a subset of MARC fields and uses language-based tags rather than numeric ones, in some cases regrouping elements from the MARC 21 bibliographic format. MODS is expressed using the XML schema language.

Natural-language-based searching—Allows users to phrase their search strings as normal sentences.

NCIP (NISO Circulation Interchange Protocol)—A protocol for the exchange of library circulation information between circulation/interlibrary loan applications and other related applications.

Nomadic computing—The use of portable computing devices (such as laptop and handheld computers) in conjunction with mobile communications technologies to enable users to access the Internet and data on their home or work computers from anywhere in the world.

OAI (Open Archives Initiative)—An organization dedicated to developing interoperability standards to facilitate the dissemination of content. www.openarchives.org

OAIS (Open Archival Information System)—A conceptual framework for a generic digital archiving system, to supply common terminology and concepts for describing and comparing data models and archival architectures; expand consensus on the elements and processes endemic to digital information preservation and access; and create a framework to guide the identification and development of standards.

OASIS (Organization for the Advancement of Structured Information Standards)—A not-for-profit consortium that leads development of e-business standards. www.oasis-open.org

OCLC FAST—To make bibliographic control systems easier to use, understand and apply, OCLC Research has modified the Library of Congress Subject Heading (LCSH) with a simpler syntax. FAST retains the very rich vocabulary of LCSH while making the schema easier to understand, control, apply and use. www.oclc.org/research/projects/fast

ONIX (Online Information eXchange)—An initiative of publishers and booksellers, ONIX is the international standard for representing and communicating book industry product information in electronic form, for Web stores and e-commerce purposes. www.editeur.org/onix.html

Ontologies—Lists of terms that provide formalized views of certain parts of the world. They explain entities within domains, their attributes and their relationships with other entities.

Open eBook—Open eBook Forum (OeBF) is a trade and standards organization dedicated to the development and promotion of electronic publishing by developing, publishing and maintaining common specifications relating to electronic books. www.openebook.org

Open source—Commonly used to refer to software that is released with its source code. The term is sometimes used interchangeably with "free software." The Open Source Initiative (www.opensource.org) Web site states that the term should be used only to describe software that has been certified by OSI.

Open source content—Open source intellectual property.

Open source databases—Open source relational databases or other structured data stores.

Open source grid engines—Open source software for distributed, and possibly multiowned, computing resource management and allocation.

Open source software—A program in which the source code is available to the general public for use and/or modification from its original design, free of charge.

OpenURL—Syntax to create Web-transportable packages of metadata and/or identifiers about an information object. Such packages are at the core of context-sensitive or open link technology. By standardizing this syntax, the OpenURL will enable many other innovative user-specific services. www.niso.org/committees/committee_ax.html

Peak of Inflated Expectations (Gartner, Inc. term)—This phase of a Hype Cycle is characterized by overenthusiasm and unrealistic projections. A flurry of well-publicized activity by technology leaders results in some successes, but more failures, as the technology is pushed to its limits. Often, the only enterprises making money during this phase are conference organizers and magazine publishers.

Personal knowledge management—Powerful knowledge management (KM) systems on the desktop that automatically adapt to usage patterns and integrate knowledge sources.

Personal knowledge networks—Virtual networks centered on individual knowledge workers that provide role-, device- and location-based connectivity and information.

Personalization (general)—Gears a system's activities (a Web site, call center or the entire enterprise) toward a user's specific information needs and preferences.

Plateau of Productivity (Gartner, Inc. term)—During this phase of a Hype Cycle, the real-world benefits of the technology are demonstrated and accepted. Tools and methodologies are increasingly stable as they enter their second and third generations. The final height of the plateau varies according to whether the technology is broadly applicable or benefits only a niche market. Approximately 30 percent of the technology's target audience have or are adopting the technology as it enters the Plateau.

Platform—In the current world of computer systems and product innovation, the platform concept generically describes a closely related family of products, technologies or computer systems. Platform implies characteristics that make the technology or product instantly recognizable within its family. A platform, accordingly, effectively serves a manufacturer as a de facto standard and plays a useful part in making the company clear and comprehensible both internally and externally.

POD—Print On Demand, a publishing model where books can be printed as they're needed by a buyer, point of sale or library.

Portal—Used in the information industries as a figurative open door through which selected, organized information passes into a defined community of users. The term has become more generalized in recent years so that it now also refers to companies or electronic systems that provide a portaling service. See also "Transparent portal" and "Vertical portal."

Portals as Web services consumers—The use of an enterprise portal to serve as the device through which the results of Web services are displayed.

Presence management—The ability to detect whether other users are online and whether they are available.

PURLs (Persistent Uniform Resource Locators)—An initiative of OCLC Research to alleviate "404 document not found" problems on the Web. A PURL is a special URL that instead of pointing directly to the location of an Internet resource points to an intermediate resolution service. The PURL resolution service associates the PURL with the actual URL and returns that URL to the client. The client can then complete the URL transaction in the normal fashion. In Web parlance, this is a standard HTTP "redirect." http://purl.org

RDF (Resource Discovery Framework)—Describes formal metadata that provides interoperability between applications that exchange information on the Web. The primary use of RDF is to enable automated processing of Web resources. www.w3.org/RDF

Real-time collaboration—Interaction between participants in real time, using a meeting or presentation format. Includes application and whiteboard sharing.

Recommender systems and personalization—The ways in which information and services can be tailored to match the unique and specific needs of an individual or a community. Recommender systems are a particular type of personalization that learn about a person's needs and then proactively identify and recommend information that meets those needs.

Records management—The management of knowledge content through its complete life cycle.

RFID (Radio frequency identification)—Applied at the unit level, RFID uses tags with data-storage capability to store manufacturing and product details. Passive tags do not require power, as they get their energy from the reader. There have been suggestions in the library literature that RFIDs will be used for collection inventories and circulation.

SCORM (Sharable Content Object Reference Model)—A suite of technical standards that enable Web-based learning systems to find, import, share, reuse and export learning content in a standardized way. www.adlnet.org

Search engine—A service that scans content on the Internet using a computer program that searches for specific keywords and returns a list of content in which they were found.

Secure Web services—Implementations of Web services that resist hacking or damage through computer attack.

Security Assertion Markup Language—A standard format specification for security assertions related to identity and authentication. Supports reduced sign-on across domains and enterprises and enables participants within a community of trust to vouch for the authentication of participants.

Semantic Web—Extends the Web through semantic markup languages, such as Resource Description Framework, Web Ontology Language and Topic Maps that describe entities and their relationships in the underlying document. www.w3.org/2001/sw

Shibboleth—A project of Internet2/MACE to develop architectures, policy structures, practical technologies and an open-source implementation in support of interinstitutional sharing of Web resources subject to access controls. In addition, Shibboleth will develop a policy framework that will allow interoperation within the higher education community. http://shibboleth.internet2.edu

Shifted Librarian—Someone who works to make libraries more portable to meet users' information needs in their world (Jenny Levine coined this term).

Slope of Enlightenment (Gartner, Inc. term)—This phase of a Hype Cycle is characterized by focused experimentation and solid hard work by an increasingly diverse range of organizations that lead to a true understanding of the technology's applicability, risks and benefits. Commercial, off-the-shelf methodologies and tools ease the development process.

Smart card—A plastic card, about the size of a credit card, that provides tamper-resistant storage of such personal information as passwords or digital signatures.

Smart enterprise suites—The convergence of portals, content management and collaboration functionality into a single product.

SOAP (Simple Object Access Protocol)—Allows one application to invoke a remote procedure call on another application or pass an object to a remote location using an XML message and the Internet. www.w3.org/TR/SOAP

Social networks—Social networking to exchange information is still one of the most popular means for obtaining information, particularly if those information needs are fuzzy. Interestingly, processes to support social networking are fairly well-known and often very cheap (e.g., "brown bag" lunches or virtual communities).

Social software—A term used to describe the application of all types of Internet-based collaborative software, from e-mail and instant messaging to Web logs.

SRW/SRU (Search and Retrieve on the Web and **Search and Retrieve with URLs)**—SRW is the protocol that aims to integrate access to various networked resources and to promote interoperability among distributed databases. It is a Web service-based protocol that builds on the Z39.50 protocol.

Tablet PC—Meets all the criteria for a notebook PC, except that it is equipped with a pen and on-screen digitizer. Tablet PCs also have removable keyboards or rotating screens that can be positioned on the outside when the lid is closed.

Taxonomy—A classification, often hierarchical, of information components (e.g., terms, concepts, graphics and sounds) and the relationships among them that support the discovery of and access to information.

Team collaboration support—Team-oriented collaboration tools that bring together real-time communications and asynchronous collaboration for team activities and tasks.

Technology Trigger (Gartner, Inc. term)—A breakthrough, public demonstration, product launch or other event that generates significant press and industry interest.

TEI (Text Encoding Initiative)—An international and interdisciplinary standard that helps libraries, museums, publishers and individual scholars represent all kinds of literary and linguistic texts for online research and teaching.

Time to Plateau/Adoption Speed (Gartner, Inc. term)—The time required for the technology to reach the Plateau of Productivity phase of the Hype Cycle.

Transparency—An intermediate step in a production or distribution process that is invisible to those who use or work in the process.

Transparent portal—An information portal, typically located between two other portals. From the other sides, it is not possible to "see" that the intermediate information portal exists. A college library that assembles and presents digitized information to students in an undergraduate course may be said to be functioning as a transparent portal, if the students are unaware that the library is involved in the process of generating, aggregating and presenting information to them through the "course portal." See also "Portal."

Trough of Disillusionment (Gartner, Inc. term)—Because the technology does not live up to its inflated expectations during this phase of a Hype Cycle, a product or service rapidly becomes unfashionable. Media interest wanes, except for a few cautionary tales.

UDDI (Universal Description, Discovery and Integration Protocol)—Provides a type of directory service for enterprises to publish, search for and use Web services. www.uddi.org

Value chain partners—Business firms or other productive agencies that have linked themselves together into a chain that is managed as one entity in a production process (even though it includes more than one company). Each step of this process creates additional value, and the total produces more value than the sum of the parts.

Vertical portal—A specialized or customized information service. In a vertical portal, selected classes and sources of information are bundled into a package that is defined by fairly clear topic boundaries. These topic boundaries are chosen to meet identified needs of the users.

Video conferencing—The process of conducting a conference between two or more participants over a network in such a way that the participants are visible. Point-to-point video conferencing involves just two participants, while multipoint video conferencing involves three or more.

Virtual community—A self-selecting, peer-to-peer group that connects people by interest, skills and practices. Virtual communities complement, but do not supersede, teams and reporting structures.

Virtual content repositories—Portals and Content Management (CM) systems that abstract access to and management of a variety of Web content, including documents, records and digital assets.

Virtual teams—A project-oriented group of knowledge workers who are not required to work in the same location or time zone.

Web-content management—Controlling Web site content through the use of specific tools. Web content management (WCM) solutions offer core functionality that goes well beyond simply managing HTML pages.

Web services—Programmatic interfaces attached to Web-based applications, supported by a suite of application-to-application communication protocols.

Web Services Description Language—A formal XML vocabulary and grammar that lets enterprises describe, discover and use Web services.

Web services enabled business models—New approaches for doing business that would not have been possible without the benefits of Web services.

"What's related" functionality—Provides a simple way of drilling down into a particular area, given that the user has already discovered a useful document (i.e., searching for "more like this"). This functionality is a basic form of personalization and there are several simple ways to implement this, e.g., by keyword search engine using "relevance feedback," by collaborative filtering or by other affinity calculations.

Whiteboard—An area on a display screen on which multiple users can write or draw. Whiteboards are a principal component of teleconferencing applications because they enable visual as well as audio communication.

Wi-Fi—Wireless fidelity refers to wireless local area networks that use one of the three 802.11 standards (802.11a, 802.11g, 802.11b).

Wiki—A Web site designed for collaborative use.

Workflow—The process whereby items of work move from one person or process to another in an organization.

WSDL (Web Services Description Language)—A formal XML vocabulary and grammar that let enterprises describe, discover and use Web services.

XML—A language designed to identify document elements and attributes in a text stream for application processing in multiple domains. Because it is plain text, users as well as computers can understand the purpose of the data if descriptive labels are used.

Xquery—A query language that supports processing of XML-based documents.

XSLT (XML Stylesheet Language Transformations)—Language for transforming XML documents in other XML document types.

Z39.50—A client/server-based protocol for searching and retrieving information across remote databases.

ZING—"Z39.50-International: Next Generation." Covers a number of initiatives (SRU, CQL, SRW, Zoom) to make the semantic content of Z39.50 more broadly available and applicable. www.loc.gov/z3950/agency/zing/zing-home.html

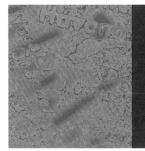

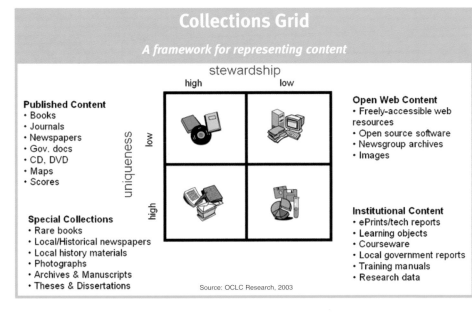

Collections Grid

A framework for representing content

stewardship
high   low

uniqueness
low
high

Published Content
• Books
• Journals
• Newspapers
• Gov. docs
• CD, DVD
• Maps
• Scores

Special Collections
• Rare books
• Local/Historical newspapers
• Local history materials
• Photographs
• Archives & Manuscripts
• Theses & Dissertations

Open Web Content
• Freely-accessible web resources
• Open source software
• Newsgroup archives
• Images

Institutional Content
• ePrints/tech reports
• Learning objects
• Courseware
• Local government reports
• Training manuals
• Research data

Source: OCLC Research, 2003

Collections Grid

Lorcan Dempsey and Eric Childress of OCLC Research developed the collections grid as a simple way to represent an increasingly complex universe. The spectrum of materials that currently comprise the actual and potential collections of libraries of all types, museums, archives and historical societies is increasingly diverse. The grid provides a spatial framework for these collections of content.

The grid divides collection materials into four general categories, each representing a distinct group of resources. The vertical axis of the grid represents the degree of "uniqueness" of the content; the horizontal axis represents "stewardship" or the degree of custodial care that the resources require.

Collection Grid Definition

Upper left quadrant. The upper left quadrant illustrates "published" information. **Published Content** includes books, magazines and newspapers, scholarly journals, government documents, CDs, DVDs/videos and published maps and scores. These materials can be either print, electronic or both.

Libraries traditionally have been focused on acquiring, managing and presenting these published resources, whether they are purchased, licensed or linked to.

Well-established practices have facilitated management of these nonunique, published materials, and mature, fully developed standards have reduced libraries' burden of metadata creation. In short, the library's role in this domain has been clear.

Upper right quadrant. The grid's upper right quadrant illustrates resources available on the Web to anyone. **Open Web Content**

includes freely accessible Web sites, open-source software, newsgroup archives and images.

Although these materials are not unique, they're not published in the traditional sense. They are likely to be unmanaged (and maybe unmanageable). Libraries' roles in acquiring, managing and presenting this content is not clear yet. Emerging standards are immature at best, and there are no established practices for collection management of these materials.

Lower left quadrant. The lower left quadrant, **Special Collections**, represents content often found in the special collections of libraries. For museums and historical societies this material comprises a substantial proportion of their collections. Content includes rare books, local and historical newspapers, local history materials, photographs, manuscripts, theses and dissertations.

Often unique, these materials are usually "high maintenance," requiring special physical environments, access (both bibliographic and physical) and preservation. Immature standards mean a high burden of metadata creation for libraries and archives.

In this domain, the institutional focus moves from acquiring, managing and distributing published materials to acting as "publisher" and curator. Since these resources "belong" to the institution, the institution's new role as knowledge creator is less clear.

Lower right quadrant. The **Institutional Content** quadrant is where, for academic libraries, learning and research materials dwell, including such resources as learning objects, courseware, e-portfolios, e-prints, technical reports and research data. For public, state or school libraries, these materials might include local

government reports, internal training manuals and tutorials, minutes of board meetings, budget reports, vertical files and so on. In a corporate library this content could include e-mail, proprietary financial reports and information, and policies and procedures.

Most institutional content is unique to the institution, and traditionally libraries have not managed it by formally collecting or by providing bibliographic control. The lack of standards, or at best the presence of very immature emerging standards, means there is a high burden of metadata creation.

Institutional content is often unpublished, but it belongs to the creators: faculty, researchers, trainers, elected officials, committees, employees and advisory boards.

Collections Grid

Interview Questions

As you consider collection management in your organization today, we would like your insights on some of the issues exposed by the grid by asking you a few questions.

1. What are major trends for materials in the Published Content quadrant?

2. What impact does the existence of materials in the Open Web, Special Collections and Institutional Content quadrants have for your library collection?

3. What are the implications for preservation and digital preservation?

4. How are the materials in the Special Collections and Institutional Content quadrants affecting your collection planning/ development?

5. How can libraries provide sustainability for the materials in the Special Collections and Institutional Content quadrants?

6. How do you see the Grid as being useful in your library planning?

People Consulted

Jessica B. Albano
Communication Studies Librarian
University of Washington
Suzzallo Library
Seattle, Washington, USA

Carolyn Anderson
Associate Director for Central Resource
  Library & Collection Development
Johnson County Library
Shawnee Mission, Kansas, USA

Chris Bailey
Director of Library Services
Glasgow University Library
Glasgow, Scotland, UK

Pam Bailey
Director
OCLC Western Service Center
Ontario, California, USA

Chris Batt
Chief Executive
The Council for Museums, Archives &
  Libraries
London, England, UK

Tim Berners-Lee
Director
World Wide Web Consortium (W3C)
Cambridge, Massachusetts, USA

Janet Bix
Librarian
Ohio Department of Transportation Library
Columbus, Ohio, USA

Phillip Blackwell
CEO
Blackwell Ltd.
Oxford, England, UK

Lydia Bower
Web Content Manager
Johnson County Public Library
Shawnee Mission, Kansas, USA

David Bradbury
Director of Libraries & Guildhall Art Gallery
Corporation of London
London, England, UK

Jo Budler
Deputy State Librarian
Library of Michigan
Lansing, Michigan, USA

Carol Bursik
Assistant Director for Access & Organization
U.S. Department of Justice Libraries
Washington, District of Columbia, USA

Susan Fifer Canby
Vice President, Libraries &
  Information Services
National Geographic Society Library
Washington, District of Columbia, USA

Kathryn Caras
Director of Electronic Publishing
Indiana University Press
Bloomington, Indiana, USA

Mona Carmack
County Librarian
Johnson County Public Library
Shawnee Mission, Kansas, USA

Warwick Cathro
Acting Deputy Director-General
National Library of Australia
Canberra, ACT, Australia

David Cohen
Associate Provost & Dean of Libraries
College of Charleston
Robert Scott Small Library
Charleston, South Carolina, USA

Patrick Coleman
Acquisitions Librarian
Minnesota Historical Society
St. Paul, Minnesota, USA

Paul Conway
Director, Information Technology Services
Duke University
William R. Perkins Library
Durham, North Carolina, USA

Lynn Copeland
University Librarian
Simon Fraser University
W A C Bennett Library
Vancouver, British Columbia, Canada

Cindy Cunningham
U.S. Catalog Librarian
Amazon
Seattle, Washington, USA

Terry Davis
President & CEO, AASLH
American Association for State and
  Local History (AASLH)
Nashville, Tennessee, USA

Deb deBruijn
Executive Director
Canadian National Site Licensing Project
Ottawa, Ontario, Canada

John Dolan
Assistant Director, Library &
  Information Services
The Library of Birmingham
Birmingham, England, UK

Ron Dunn
President & CEO, Academic &
  International Group
Thomson Corporation
Stamford, Connecticut, USA

Patrick Durando
Business Development Manager
Marcel Dekker
New York, New York, USA

Max Evans
Executive Director
National Historical Publications and Records
  Commission (NHPRC)
Washington, District of Columbia, USA

Clive Field
Director, Scholarship & Collections
British Library
London, England, UK

Terri Fredericka
Executive Director
INFOhio
Columbus, Ohio, USA

Eleanor Frierson
Deputy Director
National Agricultural Library
Washington, District of Columbia, USA

David Fuegi
Library Consultant
MDR Partners
Colchester, England, UK

Nadina Gardner
Assistant Director for Libraries & Archives,
Heritage Preservation National Institute
  for Conservation
Washington, District of Columbia, USA

Jim Gates
Director
Research Library
Baseball Hall of Fame
Cooperstown, New York, USA

Paul Gherman
University Librarian
Vanderbilt University
Jean & Alexander Heard Library
Nashville, Tennessee, USA

Mark Gilbert
Vice President and Research Director
Gartner, Inc.
Stamford, Connecticut, USA

William Gosling
Director
University of Michigan Library
Ann Arbor, Michigan, USA

Alice Grant
Alice Grant Consulting
Spalding, Lincolnshire, UK

Dan Greenstein
Executive Director
California Digital Library
Oakland, California, USA

Tommi Grover
Director of Sales & Distribution
Multilingual Matters
Clevedon, England, UK

Barbara Gubbin
Director
Houston Public Library
Houston, Texas, USA

John Haar
Associate University Librarian and
  Director, Central Llibrary
Vanderbilt University
Jean & Alexander Heard Library
Nashville, Tennessee, USA

Juha Hakala
Director, Information Technology
Helsinki University Library/National
  Library of Finland
Helsinki, Finland

Leigh Watson Healy
Vice President & Chief Analyst
Outsell, Inc.
Burlingame, California, USA

Rick Henning
Vice President
Edward Elgar Publishing, Inc.
Northampton, Massachusetts, USA

Mary Anne Hile
Collection Services Manager
Johnson County Library
Shawnee Mission, Kansas, USA

Peter Hirtle
President
Society of American Archivists
Chicago, Illinois, USA

Martin Jennings
Institute of Public Finance
Croydon, England, UK

Vickey Johnson
Director of Libraries
Sunnyvale Public Library
Sunnyvale, California, USA

Dan Jones
President
Newsbank Inc.
Naples, Florida, USA

Bonnie Juergens
Executive Director
Amigos
Dallas, Texas, USA

Anne Kenney
Associate University Librarian for Instruction,
  Research & Information Services
Cornell University Library
Ithaca, New York, USA

Erlene Bishop Killeen
District Library Media Coordinator &
  Media Director
Stoughton Area School District
Stoughton, Wisconsin, USA

Jerry Klein
Chairman & CEO
Innovative Interfaces, Inc.
Emeryville, California, USA

Rita Knox
Vice President and Research Director
Gartner, Inc.
Stamford, Connecticut, USA

Charles Kratz
Director, Library & Information Resources
University of Scranton
Harry & Jeanette Weinberg Memorial Library
Scranton, Pennsylvania, USA

Lou Latham
Knowledge Management Analyst
Gartner, Inc.
Stamford, Connecticut, USA

Madeleine Lefebvre
University Librarian
St. Mary's University
Patrick Power Library
Halifax, Nova Scotia, Canada

Dianne Leong Man
Deputy University Librarian (Technical
  Services)
University of the Witwatersrand
Wartenweiler Library
Johannesburg, South Africa

Vicki Lepine
Marketing Director
MIT Press
Cambridge, Massachusetts, USA

Jenny Levine
Internet Development Specialist
Suburban Library System
Burr Ridge, Illinois, USA

Debra Logan
Research Director
Gartner, Inc.
Stamford, Connecticut, USA

Dr. Peter Lor
National Librarian
National Library of South Africa
Consulted by Dianne Leong Man on
  OCLC's behalf
Pretoria, South Africa

Patrick Losinski
Executive Director
Columbus Metropolitan Library
Columbus, Ohio, USA

Wendy Lougee
University Librarian
University of Minnesota Libraries
Minneapolis, Minnesota, USA

Richard Lucier
Librarian of the College
Dartmouth College
Baker Library
Hanover, New Hampshire, USA

Claudia Lux
General Director
Berlin Central & Regional Library, Germany
Berlin, Germany

Cliff Lynch
Executive Director
Coalition for Networked Information
Washington, District of Columbia, USA

Mary-Alice Lynch
Executive Director
Nylink
Albany, New York, USA

Karen Danczak Lyons
First Deputy Commissioner
Chicago Public Library
Chicago, Illinois, USA

Carol Mandel
Dean of Libraries
New York University
Elmer Holmes Bobst Library
New York, New York, USA

James Marcum
University Librarian
Fairleigh Dickinson University Library
Teaneck, New Jersey, USA

Robert Martin
Director
Institute of Museum and Library Services
Washington, District of Columbia, USA

Bob Massie
Director
Chemical Abstracts Service
Columbus, Ohio, USA

Anne McFarland
Head of Technical Services
Research Library
Baseball Hall of Fame
Cooperstown, New York, USA

Esahack Mohammed
Research, Planning and Development
  Department
Office of the Executive Director
National Library And Information System
  of Trinidad and Tobago
Port of Spain, Republic of Trinidad
  and Tobago

Tom Moritz
Boeschenstein Director of Library Services
American Museum of Natural History
Washington, District of Columbia, USA

Richard Murphy
Library System Director
Prince William Public Library System (VA)
Prince William, Virginia, USA

Wendy Newman
Chief Executive Officer
Brantford Public Library,
Brantford, Ontario, Canada

Joyce Ogburn
Associate Director of Libraries For Resources
  & Collection Management Services
University of Washington Libraries
Seattle, Washington, USA

Doug Poff
Associate Director, Library Technology
  Resources & Services
University of Alberta Library
Edmonton, Alberta, Canada

Andy Powell
Assistant Director, Distributed
  Systems & Services
UKOLN
Bath, England, UK

Priscilla Ratliff
Manager
Ashland Inc. Library &
  Information Services
Dublin, Ohio, USA

Helen Ann Rawlinson
Deputy Director
Richland County Public Library
Columbia, South Carolina, USA

Norma Read
Manager, Bibliographic Access
University of Cape Town
Chancellor Oppenheimer Library
Cape Town, South Africa

Lawrence L. Reger
President
Heritage Preservation National Institute
  for Conservation
Washington, District of Columbia, USA

Julie Reilly
Associate Director & Chief Conservator
Gerald R. Ford Conservation Center/
Omaha, Nebraska, USA

Tim Rogers
Associate Director for Technology &
  Bibliographic Services
Johnson County Public Library
Shawnee Mission, Kansas, USA

Dr. Seamus Ross
Director
HATII (Humanities Advanced Technology &
  Information Institute)
Glasgow, Scotland, UK

Karen Schneider
Director
Librarians' Index to the Internet
Richmond, California, USA

Robert Seal
University Librarian
Texas Christian University
Mary Couts Burnett Library
Fort Worth, Texas, USA

Claudiu Secara
Publisher
Algora Publishing
New York, New York, USA

Merrily Taylor
University Librarian
Brown University Library
Providence, Rhode Island, USA

Roy Tennant
Manager, eScholarship Web &
  Services Design
University of California
California Digital Library
Oakland, California, USA

Sarah Thomas
C A Kroch University Librarian
Cornell University Library
Ithaca, New York, USA

Robert Usherwood
Department of Information Studies
University of Sheffield
Sheffield, England, UK

Don Waters
Program Officer
Andrew W. Mellon Foundation
New York, New York, USA

C. David Warren
Director
Richland County Public Library
Columbia, South Carolina, USA

John Warren
Marketing Director
RAND Institute
Santa Monica, California, USA

Jean Wilkins
Director
Illinois State Library
Springfield, Illinois, USA

James Williams
Dean
University of Colorado Libraries
Boulder, Colorado, USA

Ann Wolpert
Director of Libraries
Massachusetts Institute of Technology
  Libraries
Cambridge, Massachusetts, USA

Dana Yanalavich
Director of Electronic Sales, Marketing
  & Development
SUNY University Press
Albany, New York, USA

Laura Zupko
Assistant Commissioner for Collections
Chicago Public Library
Chicago, Illinois, USA

Readings & Sources

Readings

Abid, Abdelaziz. "UNESCO, Library Development and the World Summit on the Information Society." Paper presented at the World Library and Information Congress, 69th IFLA General Conference and Council, Berlin, Germany, 1–9 August 2003. www.ifla.org/IV/ifla69/papers/154e-Abid.pdf.

ACRL. *ACRL Environmental Scan 2002*. ALA: Washington, DC, 2002.

Adams, Douglas. "How to Stop Worrying and Learn to Love the Internet." This piece first appeared in the News Review section of *The Sunday Times* on August 29, 1999. www.douglasadams.com/dna/19990901-00-a.html.

Anderson, Rick. "The Library Collection and Other Moribund Concepts." *Against The Grain* 15, no. 3 (June 2003): 47–48.

Andrews, Whit and others. "Hype Cycle for Web Services, 2003." *Strategic Analysis Report*. Stamford, CT: Gartner, Inc., May 30, 2003.
> "Web services standards, such as Simple Object Access Protocol and Web Services Description Language, are understood and deployed. Application exploitation of Web services is still overhyped."

ARL Collections & Access Issues Task Force. "Collections & Access for the 21st-Century Scholar: Changing Roles of Research Libraries." *ARL Bimonthly Report* 225 (December 2002). www.arl.org/newsltr/225/.

Arevolo, W. and others. "Hype Cycle for IT in Latin America." *Strategic Analysis Report*, R-20-2997. Stamford, CT: Gartner, Inc., June 19, 2003.
> "Technology adoption in Latin American countries depends on factors that go beyond technology maturity, such as economic development, tight budgets and skills shortages."

Atkins, Daniel E., et. al. *Revolutionizing Science and Engineering Through Cyber-infrastructure*. Report of the National Science Foundation Blue Ribbon Advisory Panel on Cyberinfrastructure. January 2003. www.communitytechnology.org/nsf_ci_report/.

Batt, Chris. "Battling for Britain's Public Library Network." *Library & Information Update* 2, no. 5 (May 2003): 38–9.

Beaudiquez, Marcelle. "The Perpetuation of the National Bibliographies in the New Virtual Information Environment." Paper presented at the World Library and Information Congress, 69th IFLA General Conference and Council, Berlin, Germany, 1–9 August 2003. www.ifla.org/IV/ifla69/papers/142e_trans-Beaudiquez.pdf.

Behrens, L. and others. "Hype Cycle for Consumer Technologies." *Strategic Analysis Report*, R-19-8102. Stamford, CT: Gartner, Inc., June 6, 2003.
> "As digital technologies replace analog for consumer products, high-speed wireless bandwidth will be increasingly important to connect devices for the home."

Besser, Howard. "The Next Stage: Moving from Isolated Digital Collections to Interoperable Digital Libraries." *First Monday* 7, no. 6 (June 2002): n.p. http://firstmonday.org/issues/issue7_6/besser/.

Blechar, Michael J. "How to Manage Your Metadata." *Article Top View,* AV-20-5975. Stamford, CT: Gartner, Inc., August 18, 2003.

_____. "What is Metadata and Why Should You Care?" *Research Note,* COM-19-7824. Stamford, CT: Gartner, Inc., April 22, 2003.

Bocher, Bob. *FAQ on E-rate Compliance with the Children's Internet Protection Act and the Neighborhood Children's Internet Protection Act.* Madison, WI: Wisconsin Department of Public Instruction, August 1, 2003. www.dpi.state.wi.us/dltcl/pld/cipafaq.html.

Breeding, Marshall and Carol Roddy. "The Competition Heats Up: Automated System Marketplace 2003." *Library Journal* 128, no. 6 (April 1, 2003): 52–6, 58, 60, 62–4.

Britz, Johannes and Peter Lor. "A Moral Reflection on the Digitization of Africa's Documentary Heritage." Paper presented at the World Library and Information Congress, 69th IFLA General Conference and Council, Berlin, Germany, 1–9 August 2003. www.ifla.org/IV/ifla69/papers/146e-Britz_Lor.pdf.

Brown, John Seely. "Learning in the Digital Age." In *The Internet and the University: 2001 Forum,* edited by Maureen Devlin, Richard Larson and Joel Meyerson, 65–91. Boulder, CO: EDUCAUSE. 2002. www.educause.edu/ir/library/pdf/ffpiu015.pdf.

Caldwell, F. and others. "Hype Cycle for Knowledge Management, 2003." *Strategic Analysis Report,* R-20-0010. Stamford, CT: Gartner, Inc., June 6, 2003.
> "Content management technologies deliver business value, even in difficult economic times. Enterprises should distinguish between core technologies and emerging trends through a review of the CM hype cycle."

Callan, Jamie and others. *Personalisation and Recommender Systems in Digital Libraries.* Joint NSF-EU DELOS Working Group Report, [n.l.], May 2003. www.dli2.nsf.gov/internationalprojects/working_group_reports/personalisation.html.

Callan, Patrick M. "Coping With Recession: Public Policy, Economic Downturns, and Higher Education." In *The Ford Policy Forum 2002: Exploring the Economics of Higher Education.* Cambridge, MA: Forum for the Future of Higher Education, 2002: [17 pages]. www.educause.edu/ir/library/pdf/ffpfp0203.pdf.

Cantara, M. "Web Services Pervade Systems Integration Projects." *Research Note, Decision Framework,* DF-19-8368. Stamford, CT: Gartner, Inc., June 2, 2003.

Case, Mary M. and Prudence S. Adler. "Promoting Open Access: Developing New Strategies for Managing Copyright and Intellectual Property." *ARL Bimonthly Report* 220 (February 2002): 1–5. www.arl.org/newsltr/220/access.html.

Caudle, Dana M. "The Catalog of the Future: Integrating Electronic Resources." Paper presented at the ACRL Eleventh National Conference, Charlotte, NC, April 10–13, 2003. www.ala.org/Content/NavigationMenu/ACRL/Events_and_Conferences/caudle.PDF.

Christensen, Clayton M., Sally Aaron and William Clark. "Disruption in Education." In *The Internet and the University Forum 2001,* edited by Maureen Devlin, Richard Larson and Joel Meyerson, 19–44. Boulder, CO: EDUCAUSE, 2002. www.educause.edu/ir/library/pdf/ffpiu013.pdf.

Chui, Willy. "Grid Computing: Fulfilling the Promise of the Internet." *GridComputingPlanet.com,* June 14, 2003. www.gridcomputingplanet.com/features/article.php/2234691.

Cloete, Marian and Retha Snyman. "The Enterprise Portal—Is It Knowledge Management?" *Aslib Proceedings: New Information Perspectives* 55, no. 4 (2003): 232–42.

Cole, Jeffrey I. *The UCLA Internet Report: Surveying the Digital Future. Year Three.* Los Angeles, CA: UCLA Center for Communication Policy, February 2003. www.ccp.ucla.edu/pdf/UCLA-Internet-Report-Year-Three.pdf.

Connaway, Lynn Silipigni and Stephen R. Lawrence. "A Comparison of the Functions and Processes Associated with Identifying, Selecting, Acquiring, and Organizing Paper Books and Electronic Books." In *Learning to Make a Difference,* edited by Hugh A. Thompson, 35–45. Proceedings of the ACRL Eleventh National Conference, Charlotte, NC, April 10–13, 2003. www.ala.org/Content/NavigationMenu/ACRL/Events_and_Conferences/connaway.pdf.

Crawford, Walt. "Coping with CIPA: A Censorware Special." *Cites & Insights* 3, no. 9 (Midsummer 2003). http://cites.boisestate.edu/civ3i9.pdf.

> What libraries and newspapers said following the CIPA decision, and a summary of the key SCOTUS arguments.

_____. "The Crawford Files: Shunned and Attacked—ALA and Free Speech." *American Libraries* 34, no. 5 (May 2003): 70.

_____. "Sabo, SOAF, SOAN and More." *Cites & Insights* 3, no. 11 (September 2003): 9–17. http://cites.boisestate.edu/civ3i11.pdf.

"Croatia." *Pulman Country Report: Information on Public Libraries.* [Pulman Network, European Commission. n.p., n.d.]. www.pulmanweb.org/countries/country%20profiles/infoCroatia.htm.

D'Elia, George and Corinne Jörgensen. *Collaborations Among Public Television Stations, Public Radio Stations, Public Libraries and Museums: The Results of a National Survey.* Evanston, IL: Urban Libraries Council, January 2003. www.urbanlibraries.org/Institutional%20Survey.pdf.

_____. *National Survey of the Markets for Museums, Public Libraries, Public Television, Public Radio and their Engagement in Informal Learning Activities.* Urban Libraries Council, January 2003. www.urbanlibraries.org/markeysurvey.pdf.

Dempsey, Lorcan. "The Recombinant Library: Portals and People." *Journal of Library Administration* [in press].

_____, with contributions from a working group. "Scientific, Industrial, and Cultural Heritage: A Shared Approach; A Research Framework for Digital Libraries, Museums and Archives." *Ariadne* 22 (January 2000): n.p. www.ariadne.ac.uk/issue22/dempsey/.

> A slightly amended version of a report of the same name prepared for the European Commission's Information Society Directorate-General in the context of Fifth Framework objectives.

_____. "The Subject Gateway: Experiences and Issues Based on the Emergence of the Resource Discovery Network." *Online Information Review* 24, no. 1 (April 2000): 8–23. www.rdn.ac.uk/publications/ior-2000-02-dempsey/.

Downes, Stephen. "Public Policy, Research and Online Learning." *Ubiquity* 4, no. 25 (August 13–August 26, 2003): n.p. www.acm.org/ubiquity/views/v4i25_downes.html.

> "E-learning is more than a new way of doing the old thing. Its outcomes can't be measured by the traditional process."

Drakos, Nikos. "Hype Cycle for Open-Source Technologies." *Strategic Analysis Report,*
R-19-9528. Stamford, CT: Gartner, Inc., May 30, 2003.

> "Open-source development principles are expanding into new areas. Gartner, assesses the
> maturity of 17 open-source technologies and examines their potential to disrupt software
> markets and business relationships."

Eichert, Christof. "Librarians and Politicians Behind the Same Wheel." Paper presented at the
World Library and Information Congress, 69th IFLA General Conference and Council, Berlin,
Germany, 1–9 August 2003. www.ifla.org/IV/ifla69/papers/182e-Eichert.pdf.

Elsevier ScienceDirect. *Usability Drives Value of Bibliographic Databases.* Amsterdam,
The Netherlands: July 2003.
www.info.sciencedirect.com/content_coverage/databases/sd_bdwhitepaper.pdf.

Embrey, Teresa Ross. "You Blog, We Blog: A Guide to How Teacher-Librarians Can Use Weblogs
to Build Communication and Research Skills." *Teacher Librarian* 30, no. 2 (December 2002): 7–9.

Emerging Visions for Access in the Twenty-first Century Library. Conference Proceedings. The
Council on Library and Information Resources and the California Digital Library. Washington
DC: CLIR, August 2003. www.clir.org/pubs/abstract/pub119abst.html.

Federman, Mark. "The Cultural Paradox of the Global Village." Panel presentation on
Digitization of Information and the Future of Culture. EU-Japan Fest 10th Anniversary
Symposium on The Role of Culture in an Age of Advancing Globalization, Tokyo, Japan,
February 10–11, 2003. www.mcluhan.utoronto.ca/article_culturalparadox.htm.

_____. "Enterprise Awareness McLuhan Thinking." Keynote speech at the Information
Highways Conference, Toronto, Canada, March 25, 2003.
www.mcluhan.utoronto.ca/EnterpriseAwarenessMcLuhanThinking.pdf.

Fenn, J. "Self-Service From 2003 to 2012." *Research Note,* SPA-18-9637. Stamford, CT:
Gartner, Inc., December 3, 2002.

Fenn, J. and A. Linden. "CIO Update: Key Technology Predictions, 2003 to 2012." *Article,*
IGG-01082003-02. Stamford, CT: Gartner, Inc., January 8, 2003.

Flagg, Gordon. "California Governor Halves Statewide Funding." *American Libraries,* 34, no. 3
(March 2003): 16, 18.

_____. "Libraries Confront Budget Crisis with Cutbacks and Closures." *American Libraries* 34,
no. 2 (February 2003): 14–16, 18.

_____. "Ohio Libraries Lose State Funding for July." *American Libraries* 34, no. 4
(April 2003): 17.

_____. "Staff Shifts Roil Orlando Public Library." *American Libraries* 33, no. 9
(October 2002): 18–19.

Fogg, B.J., Cathy Soohoo and David Danielson. *How Do People Evaluate a Web Site's
Credibility? Results from a Large Study.* Yonkers, NY: Consumer WebWatch, October 29, 2002.
www.consumerwebwatch.org/news/report3_credibilityresearch/stanfordPTL_abstract.htm.

Fox, Geoffrey, Shrideep Pallickara, Marlon Pierce and David Walker. "Towards Dependable Grid
and Web Services." *Ubiquity* 4, no. 25 (August 13–August 25, 2003): n.p.
www.acm.org/ubiquity/views/v4i25_foxetal.html.

> "A proposed solution to the likely problems that will occur as service complexity increases."

Fox, Megan K. "A Library in Your Palm." *Library Journal* 17 (2003): 10.
http://libraryjournal.reviewsnews.com/index.asp?layout=articlePrint&articleID=CA286650&
publication=libraryjournal.

"France." *Pulman Country Report: Information on Public Libraries.* [Pulman Network, European Commission. n.p., n.d.]. www.pulmanweb.org/countries/country%20profiles/infoFrance.htm.

Friedlander, Amy. *Dimensions and Use of the Scholarly Information Environment: Introduction to a Data Set Assembled by the Digital Library Federation and Outsell, Inc.* Washington, D.C.: Digital Library Federation: Council on Library and Information Resources, 2002. www.clir.org/pubs/reports/pub110/contents.html.

Gemmell, Jim and others. "MyLifeBits: Fulfilling the Memex Vision." Paper presented at the ACM Multimedia Conference, Juan Les Pins, France, December 1–6, 2002. http://research.microsoft.com/~jgemmell/pubs/MyLifeBitsMM02.pdf.

"Germany." *Pulman Country Report: Information on Public Libraries.* [Pulman Network, European Commission. n.p., n.d.]. www.pulmanweb.org/countries/country%20profiles/infoGermany.htm.

Gibson, William. *Pattern Recognition.* New York: G.P. Putnam's Sons, 2003.

Gilbert, Mark and others. "Hype Cycle for Content Management." *Strategic Analysis Report,* R20-0836. Stamford, CT: Gartner, Inc., June 6, 2003.
> "Content management technologies deliver business value, even in difficult economic times. Enterprises should distinguish between core technologies and emerging trends through a review of the CM hype cycle."

Godolphin, Jocelyn. *Assessment of Organizational Options for Canadian Initiative on Digital Libraries.* Report done for the Digital Library Task Force (Library & Archives Canada) and the CIDL Steering Committee. Ottawa, ON: April 2003. www.nlc-bnc.ca/cidl/Godolphin-Report-2003-e.pdf.

Gray, Jim. *Distributed Computing Economics.* Technical Report, MSR-TR-2003-24. Redmond, WA: Microsoft Research, March 2003. ftp://ftp.research.microsoft.com/pub/tr/tr-2003-24.doc.
> "Computing economics are changing. Today there is rough price parity between (1) one database access, (2) ten bytes of network traffic, (3) 100,000 instructions, (4) 10 bytes of disk storage, and (5) a megabyte of disk bandwidth. This has implications for how one structures Internet-scale distributed computing: one puts computing as close to the data as possible in order to avoid expensive network traffic."

_____ and Alex Szalay. "Online Science: The World Wide Telescope as a Prototype for the New Computational Science." Paper presented at the International Super Computing Conference; Heidelberg, 25 June 2003; Stuttgart, 27 June 2003; Edinburgh, July 1, July 4, 2003; SF FDIS July 31, 2003. www.research.microsoft.com/%7EGray/talks/WWT_ISC_2003.pdf.

_____ and others. *Online Scientific Data Curation, Publication, and Archiving.* Technical Report, MSR-TR-2002-74. Redmond, WA: Microsoft Research, July 2002. ftp://ftp.research.microsoft.com/pub/tr/tr-2002-74.doc.

> "Science projects are data publishers. The scale and complexity of current and future science data changes the nature of the publication process. Publication is becoming a major project component. At a minimum, a project must preserve the ephemeral data it gathers. Derived data can be reconstructed from metadata, but metadata is ephemeral. Longer term, a project should expect some archive to preserve the data."

Greenstein, Daniel and Suzanne E. Thorin. *The Digital Library: A Biography.* Washington, DC.: Digital Library Federation and Council on Library and Information Resources, 2002. www.clir.org/pubs/reports/pub109/pub109.pdf.

"Grokking the Infoviz." *The Economist* (June 19, 2003): n.p. www.economist.com/PrinterFriendly.cfm?Story_ID=1841120.

Guédon, Jean-Claude. "Open Access Archives: From Scientific Plutocracy to the Republic of Science." *IFLA Journal* 29 no. 2, (2003) 129–140. www.ifla.org/V/iflaj/ij-2-2003.pdf.

Hafner, B. and others. "Hype Cycle for Networking and Communications, 2003. *Strategic Analysis Report,* R-20-0029. Stamford, CT: Gartner, Inc., May 30, 2003.

> "A wave of change continues in the networking arena. Enterprises must understand which networking technologies and services will impact their environments, and when, so they can use the changes to their advantage."

Hakala, Juha. "Future Role of (Electronic) National Bibliographies." Paper presented at the World Library and Information Congress, 69th IFLA General Conference and Council, Berlin, Germany, 1–9 August 2003. www.ifla.org/IV/ifla69/papers/155e-Hakala.pdf.

_____. "There and Back Again: From Integrated to Modular Library Systems." *The Helsinki University Library Bulletin* (2003): n.p.

Hanna, Donald E. "Building a Leadership Vision: Eleven Strategic Challenges for Higher Education." *EDUCAUSE Review* 38, no. 4 (July/August 2003): 25–34. www.educause.edu/ir/library/pdf/ERM0341.pdf.

Harnad, Stevan and others. "Mandated Online RAE CVs Linked to University eprint Archives: Enhancing UK Research Impact and Assessment." *Ariadne* 35 (March/April 2003): n.p. www.ariadne.ac.uk/issue35/harnad/.

Haycock, Ken. "Blocking Access: A Report on the Use of Internet Filters in North American Schools," in *The Bowker Annual Library and Book Trade Almanac.* New York: R.R. Bowker, 2001: 233-44.

_____. *The Crisis in Canada's School Libraries: The Case for Reform and Re-Investment.* Toronto: Association of Canadian Publishers, 2003. www.peopleforeducation.com/librarycoalition/Report03.pdf.

Henry, Chuck. [interview] "Redefining the Role of the Library." *Ubiquity* 4, no. 25 (August 13–August 26, 2003): n.p. www.acm.org/ubiquity/interviews/v4i25_henry.html.

Herz, J.C. "Gaming the System: What Higher Education Can Learn from Multiplayer Online Worlds." In *The Internet and the University: 2001 Forum.* Edited by Maureen Devlin, Richard Larson and Joel Meyerson, 169–191. Boulder, CO: EDUCAUSE, 2002. www.educause.edu/ir/library/pdf/ffpiu019.pdf.

Higher Education Information Infrastructure Advisory Committee. *Research Information Infrastructure Framework for Australian Higher Education: Report of the Department of Education, Science and Training,* November 2002. www.dest.gov.au/highered/otherpub/heiiac/report.pdf.

Himma, Kenneth Einar. "What If Libraries Really Had the 'Ideal Filter'?" *Alki* 19, no. 1 (March 2003): 29–30.

Horvat, Aleksandra. "Political Perceptions: A View from Croatia." Paper presented at the World Library and Information Congress, 69th IFLA General Conference and Council, Berlin, Germany, 1–9 August 2003. www.ifla.org/IV/ifla69/papers/162e-Horvat.pdf.

Houk, Gary and Alane Wilson. "Handcrafted or Mass Produced: What Are You Willing to Pay and What is it Worth?" *OLA Quarterly* 9, no. 1 (Spring 2003): n.p. www.olaweb.org/quarterly/quar9-1/houk.shtml.

Huang, Qunqing and Xuhuang Zhang. "Libraries as Cultural Centers in Large New Communities in Guangzhou, China." Paper presented at the World Library and Information Congress, 69th

IFLA General Conference and Council, Berlin, Germany, 1–9 August 2003.
www.ifla.org/IV/ifla69/papers/113e-Qunqing_Xuhuang.pdf.

"Hungary." *Pulman Country Report: Information on Public Libraries.* [Pulman Network,
European Commission. n.p., n.d.].
www.pulmanweb.org/countries/country%20profiles/infoHungary.htm.

Hunter, Karen. "Looking Back to Look Forward: 'Chicken Little Redux' or Strategic Lessons
Learned." 2001 Miles Conrad Memorial Lecture. Paper presented at 45th NFAIS [National
Federation of Abstracting and Information Services] Annual Conference, Philadelphia, PA,
February 27, 2001. www.nfais.org/publications/mc_lecture_2001.htm.

Iannella, Renato. "Digital Rights Management (DRM) Architectures." *D-Lib Magazine,* 7, no. 6
(June 2001): [n.p.]. www.dlib.org/dlib/june01/iannella/06iannella.html.

_____ (editor). *Digital Rights Management in the Higher Education Sector.* Brisbane, Australia:
IPR Systems Pty Ltd, 2002. www.dest.gov.au/highered/eippubs/eip02_2/eip02_2.pdf.

_____ and Peter Higgs. "Driving Content Management with Digital Rights Management." *IPR
White Papers.* Brisbane, Australia: IPS Systems Pty Ltd, 2003.
www.iprsystems.com/whitepapers/CM-DRM-WP.pdf.

_____."Rights Management: Managing the Layers of Rights and Roles in the Knowledge Based
Economy." *IPR White Papers.* Brisbane, Australia: IPR Systems Pty Ltd, January 20, 2000.
www.iprsystems.com/whitepapers/Papers/Rights_Management.pdf.

Ikoja-Odongo, J.R. "Public Library Politics: The Ugandan Perspective." Paper presented at the
World Library and Information Congress, 69th IFLA General Conference and Council, Berlin,
Germany, 1–9 August 2003. www.ifla.org/IV/ifla69/papers/171e-Ikoja-Odongo.pdf.

Institute of Museum and Library Services. *White House Conference on School Libraries.*
[Washington, D.C.]: IMLS, June 2002. www.imls.gov/pubs/whitehouse0602/whitehouse.htm.

International Federation of Library Associations and Institutions. The IFLA/FAIFE World Report
2003: Intellectual Freedom in the Information Society, Libraries and the Internet. Copenhagen:
IFLA/FAIFE: 2003.

"Italy." *Pulman Country Report: Information on Public Libraries.* [Pulman Network,
European Commission. n.p., n.d.].
www.pulmanweb.org/countries/country%20profiles/infoItaly.htm.

Jackson, Mary E. and Krisellen Maloney. "Portals, Super Discover Tools, and the New Academic
Platform: Ensuring a Collective Research Library Presence on the Web." Paper presented at the
ACRL Eleventh National Conference, Charlotte, NC, April 10–13, 2003.
www.ala.org/Content/NavigationMenu/ACRL/Events_and_Conferences/jackson.pdf.

Jacobs, J. and A. Linden. "Semantic Web Technologies Take Middleware to Next Level."
Research Note, Technology, T-17-5338. Stamford, CT: Gartner, Inc., August 20, 2002.

Johnson, Doug. "Freedom and Filters." *Library Media Connection* 21, no. 5 (February 2003): 110.

Jones, Barbara M. (compiler). *Hidden Collections, Scholarly Barriers: Creating Access to
Unprocessed Special Collections Materials in North America's Research Libraries.* A White
Paper for the Association of Research Libraries Task Force on Special Collections, June 2003.
www.arl.org/collect/spcoll/ehc/HiddenCollsWhitePaperJun6.pdf.

Jones, Steve et al. *The Internet Goes to College: How Students are Living in the Future with
Today's Technology.* Washington, DC: Pew Internet & American Life Project, 2002.
www.pewinternet.org/reports/pdfs/PIP_College_Report.pdf.

_____. *Let the Games Begin: Gaming Technology and Entertainment Among College Students.* Washington, DC: Pew Internet & American Life Project, 2003. www.pewinternet.org/reports/pdfs/PIP_College_Gaming_Reporta.pdf.

Keller, Michael A., Victoria A. Reich and Andrew C. Herkovic. "What is a Library Anymore, Anyway?" *First Monday* 8, no. 5 (May 2003): n.p. http://firstmonday.org/issues/issue8_5/keller/.

Kenney, Anne R., Nancy Y. McGovern, Ida T. Martinez and Lance J. Heidig. "Google Meets eBay: What Academic Librarians Can Learn from Alternative Information Providers." *D-Lib Magazine,* 9, no. 6 (June 2003): [n.p.] www.dlib.org/dlib/june03/kenney/06kenney.html.

Kenney, Brian. "The Future of Integrated Library Systems: An LJ Round Table." *Library Journal* 128, no. 11 (2003): 36.

King, Billie J. "Great Idea Books to Bring Librarians and Classroom Teachers Together." *Knowledge Quest* 31, no. 3, (January/February 2003): 44–5.

Kirp, David. "Outsourcing the Soul of the University." In *Forum Futures 2002: Exploring the Future of Higher Education.* Cambridge, MA : Forum for the Future of Higher Education, 2002: 56–9. www.educause.edu/ir/library/pdf/ffp0212s.pdf.

Klingenstein, Ken. "The Rise of Collaborative Tools." *EDUCAUSE Review* 38, no. 4 (July/August 2003): 60–1. www.educause.edu/ir/library/pdf/ERM0347.pdf.

Knox, Rita. "Records Management Needs Metadata and XML." *Research Note,* Technology, T-19-4669. Stamford, CT: Gartner, Inc., March 14, 2003.

Knox, Rita and others, "Hype Cycle for XML Technologies, 2003." *Strategic Analysis Report,* R-19-9727. Stamford, CT: Gartner, Inc., May 30, 2003.
> "Since 1998, XML has grown from a little-known standard to become the foundation of the Web computing infrastructure. Foundational and domain-specific XML standards are key to this evolution."

Knutsen, Unni. "Electronic National Bibliographies: State of the Art Review." Paper presented at the World Library and Information Congress, 69th IFLA General Conference and Council, Berlin, Germany, 1–9 August 2003. www.ifla.org/IV/ifla69/papers/109e-Knutsen.pdf.

Kollöffel, Joost and Arian Kaandorp. "Developing a Cost/Benefit Financial Model for Hybrid Libraries." *Serials* 16, no. 1 (March 2003): 41–9. www.info.sciencedirect.com/licensing_options/library_costbenefit.pdf.

Koper, Rob. "Combining Reusable Learning Resources and Services with Pedagogical Purposeful Units of Learning." In *Reusing Online Resources: A Sustainable Approach To E-learning,* 46–59. Edited by Allison Littlejohn, London and Sterling, VA: Kogan Page, 2003.

Kotch, Marianne. "Using the New Planning for Results Process to Create Local Standards of Library Service." *Public Libraries* 41, no. 4 (July/August 2002): 216–19.

Landgraf, Tedd. "At the Center: The Library in the Wired School." *Library Journal NetConnect* (Winter 2003): 12–14.

Lavoie, Brian F. "The Incentives to Preserve Digital Materials: Roles, Scenarios, and Economic Decision-Making." *OCLC White Paper.* Dublin, OH: April 2003. www.oclc.org/research/projects/digipres/incentives-dp.pdf.

Lee, Sandra, Gerald Brown, Constanza Mekis and Diljit Singh. "Education for School Librarians: Trends and Issues from Selected Developing Countries." Paper presented at the World Library and Information Congress, 69th IFLA General Conference and Council, Berlin, Germany, 1–9 August 2003. www.ifla.org/IV/ifla69/papers/069e-Lee_Brown_Mekis_Singh.pdf.

Lenhart, Amanda. *The Ever-Shifting Internet Population: A New Look at Internet Access and the Digital Divide*. Washington, DC: Pew Internet & American Life Project, 2003. www.pewinternet.org/reports/toc.asp?Report=88.

Levin, Douglas and Sousan Arafeh. *The Digital Disconnect: The Widening Gap Between Internet-savvy Students and their Schools*. Washington, DC: Pew Internet & American Life Project. 2002. www.pewinternet.org/reports/toc.asp?Report=67.

Library and Information Commission. *New Library: The People's Network*. London: Library and Information Commission, 1997. http://www.ukoln.ac.uk/services/lic/newlibrary/full.html.

Linden, A. "Innovative Approaches for Improving Information Supply." *Research Note, Markets,* M-14-3517. Stamford, CT: Gartner, Inc., September 4, 2001.

_____. "Innovating Information Supply." *Research Note, Markets,* M-14-3517. Stamford, CT: Gartner, Inc., September 4, 2001.

> "Information resources keep improving in volume and quality and vendors are producing more and more technologies and tools to help enterprises exploit that information."

_____. "The Semantic Web: Trying to Link the World." *Research Note, Technology,* T-14-2779. Stamford, CT: Gartner, Inc., August 30, 2001.

> "The Semantic Web is about increasingly machine-readable Web content and other data. The underlying technologies are not explicitly new, but the upcoming scale and scope of deployment offers great potential—as well as challenges."

_____. "Technology Update: Automatic Text Categorization." *Research Note, Technology,* T-18-2059. Stamford, CT: Gartner, Inc., October 29, 2002.

Linden, A. and J. Fenn. "Understanding Gartner's Hype Cycles." *Strategic Analysis Report,* R-20-1971. Stamford, CT: Gartner, Inc., May 30, 2003.

Lougee, Wendy Pradt. *Diffuse Libraries: Emergent Roles for the Research Library in the Digital Age*. Washington, DC: Council on Library and Information Resources, 2002. www.clir.org/pubs/abstract/pub108abst.html.

Lux, Claudia. "The German Library System: Structure and New Developments." *IFLA Journal* 29, no. 2 (2003): 113–28. www.ifla.org/V/iflaj/ij-2-2003.pdf.

Lyman, Peter and Hal R. Varian. *How Much Information? 2003*. Berkeley: University of California, 2003. n.p. www.sims.berkeley.edu/research/projects/how-much-info-2003/.

Lynch, Clifford A. [interview] "Check Out the New Library." *Ubiquity* 4, no. 23 (July 30–August 5, 2003): n.p. www.acm.org/ubiquity/interviews/c_lynch_1.html.

_____. "Digital Collections, Digital Libraries and the Digitization of Cultural Heritage Information." *First Monday* 7, no. 5 (May 2002): n.p. http://firstmonday.org/issues/issue7_5/lynch/.

_____. "Institutional Repositories: Essential Infrastructure for Scholarship in the Digital Age." *ARL Bimonthly Report* 226 (February 2003): 1–7. www.arl.org/newsltr/226/ir.html.

Marcum, Deanna and Amy Friedlander. "Keepers of the Crumbling Culture: What Digital Preservation Can Learn from Library History." *D-Lib Magazine* 9, no. 3 (May 2003): n.p. www.dlib.org/dlib/may03/friedlander/05friedlander.html.

Marcum, James W. "Visions: The Academic Library in 2012." *D-Lib Magazine* 9, no. 3 (May 2003): [np]. www.dlib.org/dlib/may03/marcum/05marcum.html.

Martin, Mairéad and others. "Federated Digital Rights Management: A Proposed DRM Solution for Research and Education." *D-Lib Magazine* 8, no. 7/8 (July/Aug. 2002). www.dlib.org/dlib/july02/martin/07martin.html.

Martin, Robert S. "Cooperation and Change: Archives, Libraries and Museums in the United States." Paper presented at the World Library and Information Congress, 69th IFLA General Conference and Council, Berlin, 1–9 August 2003. www.ifla.org/IV/ifla69/papers/066e-Martin.pdf.

_____. "Reaching Across Library Boundaries." In *Emerging Visions for Access in the Twenty-first Century Library.* Council on Library and Information Resources and the California Digital Library. Washington DC: CLIR, August 2003: 3–16. www.clir.org/pubs/abstract/pub119abst.html.

Messerschmitt, David G. "Opportunities for Research Libraries in the NSF Cyberinfrastructure Program." *ARL Bimonthly Report* 229 (August 2003): 1–7. www.arl.org/newsltr/229/cyber.html.

Miller, Jack. *America's Most Literate Cities.* Whitewater, WI: University of Wisconsin–Whitewater, 2003. www.uww.edu/cities/fullpaper.pdf.

Minkel, Walter. "2002's Top Tech Trends." *School Library Journal* 47, no. 12 (Dec. 2001): 25–6. http://slj.reviewsnews.com/index.asp?layout=articlePrint&articleID=CA184203.

_____. "Creating an Indie Site." *School Library Journal* 49, no. 1 (Jan. 2003): 33.

_____. "Pew Study: Students Prefer Virtual Library." *School Library Journal* 48, no. 10 (October 2002): 28–30.

Moahi, Kgomotso H. "Providing Library Services in the Digital Era: Opportunities and Threats for Libraries in Africa." Paper presented at the World Library and Information Congress, 69th IFLA General Conference and Council, Berlin, 1–9 August 2003. www.ifla.org/IV/ifla69/papers/097e-Moahi.pdf.

Molholm, Kurt. "Is What's Past, Prologue?" 2003 Miles Conrad Memorial Lecture. Paper presented at the 45th NFAIS [National Federation of Abstracting and Information Services] Annual Conference, Philadelphia, PA, February 25, 2003. www.nfais.org/publications/mc_lecture_2003.htm.

Moyer, Mary. "Pluses, Minuses, and Interesting Thoughts on Using a Library Web Page with High School Students." *Library Media Connection* 21, no. 7 (April/May 2003): 50.

Mutch, Andrew and Karen Ventura. "The Promise of Internet2." *NetConnect* (Summer 2003): 14–6. www.schoollibraryjournal.com/index.asp?layout=netconnectTOC&pubdate=7/15/03.

National Science Foundation. *Post Digital Library Futures.* Invitational Workshop. Chatham, MA: June 15–17, 2003. www.sis.pitt.edu/~dlwkshop/papers.html.

> "The background papers and other materials (some presentations from the conference, breakout reports, etc.) are up on the conference Web site, and provide a fascinating spectrum of perspectives on the potential future research agendas for digital libraries and a host of related technologies."—Clifford Lynch

"The Netherlands." *Pulman Country Report: Information on Public Libraries.* [Pulman Network, European Commission. n.p., n.d.]. www.pulmanweb.org/countries/country%20profiles/infoNetherlands.htm.

Nichols, Stephen G. and Abby Smith. *The Evidence in Hand: Report of the Task Force on the Artifact in Library Collections.* Washington, DC: Council on Library and Information Resources, 2001. www.clir.org/pubs/reports/pub103/contents.html.

Nielsen, Jakob. "Information Foraging: Why Google Makes People Leave Your Site Faster." *Alertbox* (online newsletter), June 30, 2003. www.useit.com/alertbox/20030630.html.

Oblinger, Diana. "Boomers, Gen-Xers, and Millennials: Understanding the 'New Students'"
EDUCAUSE Review 38, no. 4 (July/August 2003): 37–47.
www.educause.edu/ir/library/pdf/ERM0342.pdf.

OCLC. "How Academic Librarians Can Influence Students' Web-Based Information Choices."
OCLC White Paper on *The Information Habits of College Students,* June 2002.
http://www5.oclc.org/downloads/community/informationhabits.pdf.

_____. "Five-Year Information Format Trends." *OCLC Reports.* March 2003.
http://www5.oclc.org/downloads/community/informationtrends.pdf.

OCLC E-learning Task Force (Neil MacLean and Heidi Sander, primary editors). *Libraries and the Enhancement of E-learning.* Dublin, OH: OCLC, 2003.
http://www5.oclc.org/downloads/community/elearning.pdf.

Oder, Norman and Michael Rogers. "States, Localities Cut PL Budgets." *Library Journal* 128,
no. 6 (April 1, 2003): 20, 22–3.

O'Neill, Edward T., Brian F. Lavoie and Rick Bennett. "Trends in the Evolution of the Public Web:
1998–2002." *D-Lib Magazine* 9, no. 4 (April 2003): n.p.
www.dlib.org/dlib/april03/lavoie/04lavoie.html.

Outsell, Inc. "Academic I-AIM: An Executive Summary for Information About Information
Clients." *Information Briefing* 5, no. 52 (November 20, 2002).

_____. "The Changing Roles of Content Deployment Functions: Market, Business, and
Competitive Intelligence Professionals." *Information Briefing* 6, no. 17 (July 25, 2003).

_____. "Company Assessment: Google—The Premium Fuel Search Engine." *Information
Briefing* 6, no. 16 (July 11, 2003).

_____. "TrendAlert: XML and Web Services—The Asteroids that Will Blow Up 500 Years
of Publishing History." *Information Briefing* 6, no. 15 (June 20, 2003).

Owens, Susan R. "Revolution or evolution? A shift to an open-access model of publishing
would clearly benefit science, but who should pay?" *EMBO Reports* 4, no. 8 (2003): 741–3.
www.nature.com/cgi-taf/DynaPage.taf?file=/embor/journal/v4/n8/full/
embor913.html&filetype=pdf.

Pateman, John. "Cultural Revolution." *Library & Information Update* 1, no. 1 (April 2002): 42–3.

Pearce, Liz. *Institutional Portals: A Review of Outputs.* UKOLN. June 26, 2003.
www.fair-portal.hull.ac.uk/downloads/iportaloutputs.pdf.

Phifer, G. and others. "Hype Cycle for Portal Ecosystems, 2003." *Strategic Analysis Report,*
R-20-0833. Stamford, CT: Gartner, Inc., June 6, 2003.

Pinto, Francisco and Michael Fraser. "Access Management, the Key to a Portal." *Ariadne* 35
(March/April 2003): [n.p.]. www.ariadne.ac.uk/issue35/SPP/.

Poissenot, Claude. "What is Culture According to Librarians? Is it Evidence-Based?" Paper
presented at the World Library and Information Congress, 69th IFLA General Conference and
Council, Berlin, Germany, 1–9 August 2003.
www.ifla.org/IV/ifla69/papers/104e-Poissenot.pdf.

Powell, Andy. "Mapping the JISC IE Service Landscape." *Ariadne* 36 (July 2003): n.p.
www.ariadne.ac.uk/issue36/powell/.

Prabha, Chandra and Raymond Irwin. "Web Technology in Public Libraries: Findings from Research." *Library Hi Tech* 21, no. 1 (2003): 62–9.

Prentice, S. "Regional Hype Cycle Variations: Europe, Middle East, Africa." *Research Note, Decision Framework,* DR-19-9829. Stamford, CT: Gartner, Inc., June 19, 2003.
> "Regional variations in technology adoption in EMEA can't be adequately explained by economic or infrastructure differences, or national characteristics. Other factors must be considered, such as history and culture."

Radford, Gary P. "Flaubert, Foucault, and Bibliotheque Fantastique: Toward a Postmodern Epistemology for Library Science." *Library Trends* 46, no. 4 (1998): 616–34.

Redman, P. "Hype Cycle for Mobile and Wireless Networking, 2003." *Strategic Analysis Report,* R-20-0115. Stamford, CT: Gartner, Inc., May 30, 2003.
> "Some wireless applications and services, like Short Message Service and wireless e-mail, have already been shown to improve productivity and should be embraced. Others are headed for obsolescence (wireless Web) and should be avoided."

Relyea, Harold and L. Elaine Halchin. "Homeland Security and Information Management." In *The Bowker Annual of Library and Book Trade Information* Medford, NJ: Information Today, 2003: 231–50.

Riedling, Ann Marlow. "Convincing Others of What You Can Do." *Teacher Librarian* 30, no. 4 (April 2003): 55–7.

Robb, Drew. "Collaboration Gets It Together." *Computerworld Executive Bulletin.* www.computerworld.com/softwaretopics/software/groupware/story/0,10801,76490,00.html.

St. Lifer, Evan. "Filtering and Local Control." *School Library Journal* 49, no. 1, (January 2003): 11.

Samuelson, Pamela. "Mapping the Digital Public Domain: Threats and Opportunities." *Law and Contemporary Problems* 66, no 1/2 (Winter/Spring 2003): n.p. www.law.duke.edu/shell/cite.pl?66+Law+&+Contemp.+Probs.+147+(WinterSpring+2003).

Schonfeld, Erick. "Microsoft's Latest Take on the Desktop." Business 2.0 (July 2003): n.p.

SCONUL [Society of College, National and University Libraries] and UK eUniversities Worldwide. "Information Support for eLearning: Principles and Practice." *UkeU Briefing Paper.* London: SCONUL and UK eUniversities Worldwide, 2003. www.sconul.ac.uk/pubs_stats/pubs/Information_Support_for_eLearning_Final.pdf.

Seaman, David. "Deep Sharing: A Case for the Federated Digital Library." *EDUCAUSE Review* 38, no. 4 (July/August 2003): 10–11. www.educause.edu/ir/library/pdf/ERM0348.pdf.

Shank, John D. and Nancy H. Dewald. "Establishing Our Presence in Courseware: Adding Library Services to the Virtual Classroom." *Information Technology and Libraries* 22, no. 1 (March 2003): n.p. www.ala.org/Content/NavigationMenu/LITA/LITA_Publications4/ITAL__Information_Technology_and_Libraries/2201_Shank.htm.

Sheketoff, Emily and Mary R. Costabile. "Legislation and Regulations Affecting Libraries in 2002." In *The Bowker Annual of Library and Book Trade Information*. Medford, NJ: Information Today, 2003: 305–20.

Shoniregun, Charles A. and Sarah-Jane Gray. "Is E-learning Really the Future or a Risk?" *Ubiquity* 4, no. 10 (April 29–May 5, 2003): n.p. www.acm.org/ubiquity/views/c_shoniregun_3.pdf.

Shumaker, John W. "The Higher Education Environment and the Role of the Academic Library." Paper presented at the ACRL Eleventh National Conference, Charlotte, NC, April 10–13, 2003. www.ala.org/Content/NavigationMenu/ACRL/Events_and_Conferences/shumaker.PDF.

"Slovenia." *Pulman Country Report: Information on Public Libraries.* [Pulman Network, European Commission. n.p., n.d.]. www.pulmanweb.org/countries/country%20profiles/infoslovenia.htm.

Smith, Abby. *Building and Sustaining Digital Collections: Models for Libraries and Museums.* Washington, DC: Council on Libraries and Information Resources, 2001. www.clir.org/pubs/reports/pub100/contents.html.

_____. "Issues in Sustainability: Creating Value for Online Users." *First Monday* 8, no. 5 (May 2003): [n.p.]. http://firstmonday.dk/issues/issue8_5/smith/.

_____. *New-Model Scholarship: How Will it Survive?* Washington, DC: Council on Libraries and Information Resources, 2003. www.clir.org/pubs/reports/pub114/pub114.pdf.

_____. *Strategies for Building Digitized Collections.* Washington, DC: Digital Library Federation, Council on Library and Information Resources, 2001. www.clir.org/pubs/reports/pub101/pub101.pdf.

"Spain." *Pulman Country Report: Information on Public Libraries.* [Pulman Network, European Commission. n.p., n.d.]. www.pulmanweb.org/countries/country%20profiles/infoSpain.htm.

Spooner, Tom and others. *Internet Use by Region in the United States.* Washington, DC: Pew Internet & American Life Project, 2003. www.pewinternet.org/reports/pdfs/PIP_Regional_Report_Aug_2003.pdf.

Stanton, Robin. "Toward Supported 'Communities of Interest' in Digital Environments." In *Emerging Visions for Access in the Twenty-first Century Library* 33–43, Council on Library and Information Resources and the California Digital Library. Washington DC: CLIR, August 2003. www.clir.org/pubs/abstract/pub119abst.html.

Storey, Tom. "An Interview with Herbert Van de Sompel: Developing New Protocols to Support and Connect Digital Libraries." *OCLC Newsletter* No. 261 (July 2003): 12–14. www.oclc.org/news/publications/newsletters/oclc/2003/261/n261.pdf.

_____. "University Repositories: An Extension of the Library Cooperative." *OCLC Newsletter* No. 261 (July 2003): 7–11. www.oclc.org/news/publications/newsletters/oclc/2003/261/n261.pdf.

Strategic Planning Committee. *Final Report: Environmental Scan 2001–2002.* Huntsville, TX: Sam Houston State University, 2001. www.shsu.edu/~sacs/spcreport/environmental_scan.html.

Strong, Gary E. "Libraries Empower People to Participate in a Civil Society." In *Emerging Visions for Access in the Twenty-first Century Library* 27–32, Council on Library and Information Resources and the California Digital Library. Washington DC: CLIR, August 2003. www.clir.org/pubs/abstract/pub119abst.html.

Sun Microsystems, Inc. "Digital Library Technology Trends." August, 2002. www.sun.com/products-n-solutions/edu/whitepapers/pdf/digital_library_trends.pdf.

Thirunarayanan, M.O. "From Thinkers to Clickers: The World Wide Web and the Transformation of the Essence of Being Human." *Ubiquity* 4, no. 12 (May 13–19, 2003): n.p. www.acm.org/ubiquity/views/pf/m_thirunarayanan_8.html.

"United Kingdom." *Pulman Country Report: Information on Public Libraries.* [Pulman Network, European Commission. n.p., n.d.]. www.pulmanweb.org/countries/country%20profiles/infoUK.htm.

United States Department of Commerce. A *Nation Online: How Americans are Expanding Their Use of the Internet.* Washington, DC: U.S. Dept. of Commerce. National Telecommunications and Information Administration; Economics and Statistics Administration, February 2002. www.ntia.doc.gov/ntiahome/dn/anationonline2.pdf.

University of California Libraries' Collection Management Initiative. *Preliminary Results from the Collection Management Initiative's Journal Use Study and User Preference Survey,* April 18, 2003. www.slp.ucop.edu/consultation/slasiac/042903/CMI_SurveyResultsForSLASIAC04-29-03.doc.

Unsworth, John M. "The Crisis in Scholarly Publishing in the Humanities." *ARL Bimonthly Report* 228 (June 2003): n.p. www.arl.org/newsltr/228/crisis.html.

> "These remarks were presented at the 2003 Annual Meeting of the American Council of Learned Societies (ACLS) in a session on 'Crises and Opportunities: The Futures of Scholarly Publishing.' The papers from the meeting are available on the ACLS Web site ⟨http://www.acls.org/ex-03am.htm⟩."

Van de Sompel, Herbert. "Roadblocks." Paper presented at NSF Post Digital Library Futures Workshop. (Chatham, MA: June 15–17, 2003). www.sis.pitt.edu/~dlwkshop/paper_sompel.html.

> "I have concentrated on trying to identify roadblocks in the DL arena [...] The items I identify are situated at the level of basic plumbing—things that need to be in place so that other great things can happen. Therefore, they may not come across as all that exciting or innovative, however, I feel that failing to address them may seriously impede efforts to move towards an integrated scholarly knowledge environment..."

_____, Jeffrey A. Young and Thomas B. Hickey, "Using the OAI-PMH ... Differently." *D-Lib Magazine* 9, no. 7/8 (July/August 2003). www.dlib.org/dlib/july03/young/07young.html.

Waters, Donald. "Developing Digital Libraries: Four Principles for Higher Education." *EDUCAUSE Review* 36 (September/October, 2001): 58–9. www.educause.edu/ir/library/pdf/ERM0158.pdf.

West, Jessamyn. "Google Answers is *Not* the Answer." *American Libraries* 34, no. 6 (June/July 2003): 54–6.

Wheatman, V. and others. "Hype Cycle for Information Security, 2003." *Strategic Analyst Report,* R-19-9974. Stamford, CT: Gartner, Inc., May 30, 2003.

Wilson, Betsy. *From Vision to Transformation: New Models of Academic Support for Digital Scholarship.* Project Report to the Andrew W. Mellon Foundation, July 14, 2003 [unpublished].

Young, Jeffrey R. "'Superarchives' Could Hold All Scholarly Output." *The Chronicle of Higher Education* 48, no. 43 (July 5, 2002): n.p. http://chronicle.com/free/v48/i43/43a02901.htm.

Young, Terence E., Jr. "No Pain, No Gain: The Science Teacher and You Working Together." *Library Media Connection* 21, no. 4 (January 2003): 14–21.

Sources

The Social Landscape

The Collaboration Technology Fabric p. 12

The technologies mapped to this grid were researched and identified by OCLC market analysts using the following resources:

Amazon.com (www.amazon.com) August 2003.

Google (www.google.com) July 2003.

IBM (www.ibm.com) July 2003.

Microsoft Corporation (www.microsoft.com) July 2003.

Yahoo! (www.yahoo.com) July 2003.

"Collaboration Technologies," *Computerworld Executive Bulletin* (2003).
  https://store.computerworld.com/product_pdf_summary/eb_collaboration_summ.pdf.

The Economic Landscape

The public and public goods p. 15

U.S. Bureau of the Census
  www.census.gov/ipc/www/worldpop.html, July 2003.
  www.census.gov/ipc/www/idbnew.html July 2003.
Unesco Statistical Yearbook (1999).
International Handbook of Universities (2003).
World List of Universities & Other Institutions of Higher Education (2002).
Defense and Foreign Affairs Handbook (2002).
The Center for Defense Information
  www.cdi.org/issues/wme/spendersfy03.html, February 2002.
World Health Organization (2003).
Government Finance Statistics Yearbook 2002 (IMF), January 2003.
OCLC Library & Information Center—worldwide library counts.

Library Funds—Sources and Uses pp. 18–24

Unesco. *Statistical Yearbook,* 1999. Paris.

ARL Statistics 2001–02. Association of Research Libraries, 2003, p. 5.
ARL Supplementary Statistics 2001–02. Association of Research Libraries, 2003, p. 5.

LibEcon.org: *A Research Study in International Library Economics,* Institute of Public Finance, United Kingdom, www.libecon.org/default.asp, accessed August 2003. Data used were the 2000 Grossed Estimates.

Wedgeworth, Robert, ed. *World encyclopedia of library and information services*. Chicago: American Library Association, c1993.

European Commission, The Pulman Network. *Croatia: Pulman Country Report,* www.pulmanweb.org/countries/Croatia.htm, accessed September 2003.

Notes: estimates for Brazil, Chile, China, Colombia, Croatia, Malaysia, Saudi Arabia, United Arab Emirates, and Uganda based on partial data for limited segments within each of these countries.

When possible, school libraries were omitted from library expenditure estimates. In some countries, expenditures for school libraries may be included.

Library Landscape

Top ten languages p. 76
World Almanac 2004, p.626 provided the list of top ten languages expressed as numbers. OCLC staff converted these numbers to percentages of the total world population, estimated at 6.3B.

Online language population p. 76
Global Reach. "Global Internet Statistics (by Language)." Sept 2003. www.glreach.com/globstats/.

"Here are the latest estimated figures of the number of people online in each language zone (native speakers). We classify by languages instead of by countries, since people speaking the same language form their own online community no matter what country they happen to live in."

Languages of Web content p. 76
Global Reach. "Chart of Web content, by language." Source: Vilaweb.com, as quoted by eMarketer (2003) www.glreach.com/globstats/.

WITHDRAWAL

Notes & Ideas